INTRODUCTION TO ENTREPRENEURIAL SKILLS I

Kayode Asoga-Allen

Copyright © 2016 by Kayode Asoga-Allen

All rights reserved. This book or any portion thereof may not be reproduced or used in any manner whatsoever without the express written permission of the publisher except for the use of brief quotations in a book review or scholarly journal.

First Printing: 2015

ISBN: 978-1535259149

www.kayodeasogaallen.com

DEDICATION

This book is dedicated to Almighty God, the giver of knowledge, the Creator of heaven and earth and all that are in it, Omnipotent, Omnipresent and Omniscience, for making it possible for me to make exploit on earth.

No one can receive anything on earth except it is given to him from heaven, I am grateful to God for considering me worthy and destined me among those who will make impact in this world. Human beings have tried to put the light off, but this light is from God therefore, it is unquenchable. Glory and honour be to His holy name.

Praise God, Hallelujah.

PREFACE

The course "Entrepreneurial Skills" was introduced into the curriculum of Nigerian higher institutions of learning to proffer solution to the problem of unemployment facing the graduates of our higher institutions. Unemployment has become a national issue today in Nigeria; graduates of many years who have not tested any work are found everywhere. Most of these graduates have no skill in any occupation, thus they found it difficult to earn a living.

In most advanced countries of the world, the government has the statistics of yearly admissions into the higher institutions as well as yearly output of graduates. This enables the government to pursue vigorously the creation of jobs for the graduates. In Nigeria, that is not the case, the government at all levels seems not to bother whether graduates from our institutions are employed or not. No wonder, millions of Nigerian youths are jobless.

The economy of the nation, if well managed, is capable of providing employment for all the citizens, but politics is an impoverish game, the way its played in Nigeria. The focus of most Nigerian politicians is how to corruptly enrich oneself.
Some past rulers of the nation are richer than even the nation that they ruled. Thus, politics is do or die in Nigeria,

because politics is the only business you can do to become overnight millionaire and billionaire. The level of corrupt practices of Nigerian politicians has created a serious problem of unemployment, poverty and penury for the citizens.

It is believed that with the introduction of this course "Entrepreneurial skills" students would be imparted with the skills necessary for establishing their own businesses after graduation, and be less dependent on government for a job. This book titled "Introduction to Entrepreneurial skills" have been written to cater for the students and general public who wish to become successful businessman and woman also, who desires to become an employer of labour in future rather than waste scarce time looking for unavailable job.

The content and ideas contained in this book would be of innumerable and inestimable value to the readers, most of the examples originated from the practical experience of the author as someone who has lectured the course for more than six years. Thus, I congratulate both the students of this course and the general public for the emergence of new ideas in the field of entrepreneurship.

Wishing all the prospective readers of this book, the best in their endeavours.

Kayode Asoga-Allen
B.A.(Ed.), M.Ed. Ph.D in view

Table of Contents

Copyright © 2016 by Kayode Asoga-Allen	2
DEDICATION	3
PREFACE	4
CHAPTER ONE: ENTREPRENEURSHIP	**13**
1.1 What is Entrepreneurship?	13
1.2 What role does Entrepreneur play in the Economy?	14
1.3 What are the pains and pleasures, the benefits and disadvantages of entrepreneurship?	16
1.4 What are the Characteristics of Entrepreneurship?	17
1.5 Determinants of Entrepreneurship	20
1.6 Implications of the Behavioural Analysis	21
1.7 How does one become an Entrepreneur?	21
CHAPTER TWO: ENTREPRENEURSHIP IN THEORY AND FRACTURE	**24**
2.1 What is a theory?	24
2.2 Theories of Entrepreneurship and Entrepreneurial Motivation	24
2.3 Economic Theory	24
2.4 Sociological Theory	25
2.5 Psychological Theory	25

2.6 Entrepreneurship Innovation Theory   26

2.7 Theory of High Achievement/Theory of Achievement
Motivation   27

2.8 Motivation Theory by Mcclelland (acquired needs
theory)   27

2.9 The Rakinada Experiment   27

2.10 Conclusion of the Experiment   28

CHAPTER THREE: OPPORTUNITY   29

3.1 Definition   29

3.2 Requirements to Spot Viable Business Opportunities in
Nigeria   30

3.3 The Face of Business Opportunities   31

3.4 Drivers of Opportunity   32

3.5 Failures of Existing Companies and Businesses   34

3.6 What to Consider When You Weigh the Options   34

3.7 Where to look   35

CHAPTER FOUR: FORMS OF BUSINESS   37

4.1 Sole Proprietorship   37

4.2 Advantages of Sole Proprietorship   37

4.3 Disadvantages of Sole Proprietorship   38

4.4 Partnership   38

4.5 Advantages of Partnership	39
4.6 Disadvantages of Partnership	39
4.7 Types of Partnership	39
4.8 Corporation	41
4.9 Advantages of Corporation	42
4.10 Disadvantages of Corporation	42
4.11 Cooperative Society	43
CHAPTER FIVE: STAFFING	**47**
5.1 Introduction	47
5.2 Internal Factors Affecting Staffing	47
5.2 External Factors Affecting Staffing	49
5.3 How to Get Quality Staff into Your Business	51
CHAPTER SIX: MANAGEMENT AND ADMINISTRATION OF SMALL AND MEDIUM SCALE BUSINESSES	**55**
6.1 Introduction	55
6.2 The Future of Business and Succession Issue	58
CHAPTER SEVEN: MARKETING AND MARKETING SEGMENT	**63**
7.1 Introduction	63
7.2 The Functions of Marketing	63

7.3 The Objectives of Marketing	64
7.4 Partial Analysis of the Marketing Mix: Product	65
7.5 Analyzing Products:	66
7.6 The product range	67
7.7 New product development	67
7.8 Idea generation	68
CHAPTER EIGHT: INSURANCE	69
8.1 Meaning of Insurance	69
8.2 What is Business Insurance?	69
8.3 Preparing to Purchase Insurance	71
8.4 Principles	73
8.5 Insurability	74
8.6 Legal	77
8.7 Indemnification	79
8.8 Societal Effects	81
8.9 Insurers' Business Model	82
8.10 Claims	85
8.11 Marketing	87
8.9.4 Types of Business Insurance	87

CHAPTER NINE: FEASIBILITY STUDY	96
9.1 Definition	96
9.2 Objective and Unbiased	96
9.3 Five Common Factors	97
9.4 Technical and System Feasibility	97
9.5 Legal Feasibility	98
9.6 Operational Feasibility	98
9.7 Schedule Feasibility	98
9.8 Market and Real Estate Feasibility	99
9.9 Resources Feasibility	99
9.10 Cultural feasibility	99
9.11 Market Research Study and Analysis	101
9.12 Importance of Feasibility Studies	101
9.13 Preparation of Feasibility Studies	103
9.14 The Contents of a Feasibility Report	103
9.15 Purpose of the Project	104
9.16 The Objective and Scope	104
9.17 The Business	104
9.18 The Project	105

9.19 Land and Location	105
9.20 Operational Plan	106
9.21 Desirability of the Project	107
9.22 Demand and Supply Outlook	107
9.23 Management and Manpower Requirement	107
9.24 Salaries and Benefits	108
9.25 Administrative Expenses	108
9.26 Production Cost	109
9.27 Financial Plan	109
9.28 Marketing Strategy	112
9.29 The Projects General Appraisal	113
9.30 Project Evaluation Techniques	114
CHAPTER TEN: TECHNOLOGY	115
10.1 What is Technology?	115
10.2 Technology and the Need of Man	115
Case Studies	119
10.3 Aspect of Technology Necessary for Production	120
REFERENCES	123
Index	126

CHAPTER ONE: ENTREPRENEURSHIP

In this chapter attempt shall be made to answer a few questions relating to the entire entrepreneurship. The principal questions which will be discussed in this section are:

i) What does entrepreneurship means? Or who is an entrepreneur?
ii) What role does an entrepreneur play in the economy?
iii) What are the pains and pleasures, the benefits and disadvantages of entrepreneurship?
iv) What are the characteristics of entrepreneurship? And
v) How does one become an entrepreneur?

1.1 What is Entrepreneurship?

Entrepreneurship can be defined in various ways depending on the perspective of the scholar defining it. For example, entrepreneurship can be defined as the creative ability to perceive business opportunities involving risk taking, and mobilize resources required to produce goods and services. It can also be defined as practical creativeness which combines resources and opportunities in new ways that have not been attempted before or to exploit what was previously neglected or wrest its resources from established less productive resources.

The entrepreneur is a person or group of persons either from scratch or as an outgrowth from an existing organization. An enterprise organization is a system of continuous interaction of people with land, money (capital), machine, materials, physical structures and ideas generated by the entrepreneur. The purpose of the interaction is to produce wealth through specific products and services for society. Entrepreneurs are generally found as owners (and often managers as well) of small-scale enterprises rather than in larger well-established ones. The small business is thus the "natural habitat" or the "seed base" for entrepreneurs.

1.2 What role does Entrepreneur play in the Economy?

The entrepreneur mobilizes resources and transforms them into need-satisfying goods and services through the application of management, scientific and technical knowledge developed or adapted by them. Entrepreneurs thus aid economic development through their activities which include:

- The development of new products or services from local latent resources;
- The development of new technology to suit local conditions;
- The adaptations of existing product or technology to suit local conditions;
- Commercializing existing scientific and or technological knowledge.

The entrepreneur needs a conducive environment for effectiveness. Such an environment implies political stability; policy stability and predictableness, government supportive role in terms of fiscal monetary and human resource policies, adequate infrastructural facilities, extension services in technology and management skills to mention a few.

Entrepreneurs are thus indispensable for a country's economic development, self-reliance, employment generation and general level of well being. Entrepreneurs through their activities create jobs, promote economic development and thereby increase the welfare of the general populace.

1.3 What are the pains and pleasures, the benefits and disadvantages of entrepreneurship?

As earlier mentioned, an entrepreneur is a risk-taker and a general, the higher the level of risk involved in a venture, the higher the potential for profit. Risk and profit thus present the pain and pleasure of entrepreneurship. Thus compared with paid employment, being an entrepreneur involves such pleasures as:

1) **Independence**: freedom to choose type, time and volume of work. The entrepreneur dances to his own tune and his own master.

2) **Social prestige and recognition**: A successful entrepreneur is usually highly regarded in the society. They are courted by politicians, military and even educational and other social institutions.

3) **Higher income**: Successful entrepreneurs are definitely going to be better-off than most paid employees.

4) **Sense of accomplishment**: Being an entrepreneur gives one a sense of achievement and pride, in being able to help others earn a living, or increasing the welfare of one's community.

5) **Opportunity for growth**: many of today's big businesses started small and then grew. The opportunity to grow poses a challenge to the entrepreneurs.
6) **Worldwide exposure**: Entrepreneurs often meet people from other parts of the world. They also travel to other countries very often. This experience can be exciting and pleasant.

Disadvantages

a) **Risk of failure and loss of property:** Wrong decision often result in failure
b) **Long hours of work**: No defined hour of work, no defined schedule of duties. One does what needs to be done for as long as one can.
c) **Instability or uncertainty**: Business is subject to fluctuations ups and downs. No steady flow but jerks in income/fortune.

1.4 What are the Characteristics of Entrepreneurship?

The characteristics of entrepreneurship could be interpreted to mean those attributes of an entrepreneur which distinguishes him from other people. Behavioural studies have indentified the following in western countries:

Value	(1) Achievement; (2) risk taking; (3) Imaginative; (4) initiative; (5) Leadership; (6) self-confidence; (7) Persevering, aggressive indomitable spirit.
Skills area	(8) Technical skill and competence in some (9) Management enterprise, especially Organizing ability and decision making.
Convert Behaviours	(10) Rich in ideas (11) Does things: doer of action (12) Likes to work on task with calculated risks. (13) Prefer tasks where feedback is available (14) Plan ahead with a large term view. (15) Innovative in business.

The list is by no means exhaustive. We have again selected those we consider absolutely essential features in what some behaviourist may describe as the entrepreneurs personality. The pictures emerging from the analysis of entrepreneurship thus far suggesting that development though possible is not a light matter.

In fact Collins and Moore's (1964), study further compounds the problem. They define three stages in the "organizations making" process, these include:

(1) Graduation from the "school for entrepreneurs". This stage includes the whole childhood experience marked with crises, occupational difficulties where the person moves from job to job. ("Drifting") and a kind of apprenticeship. All these combine the technical, interpersonal and management skills needed for entrepreneurship.

(2) The second "projecting phase" sees the birth of business ideas on inventions, new product, resource exploitation, new market outlet. Authors found that this phase was often triggers off by what they call "role deterioration" evident in block mobility or unemployment to cite a few examples. The state of shattered world leads budding entrepreneurs to generate business ideas.

(3) The third phase is the actual creation of organizations. Three sub-phases are also recognized. These include:

a. Gathering and organizing resources to set up an organization

b. Battling through the limited teething problems.
c. Re-organization for effective management.

1.5 Determinants of Entrepreneurship

Other question behavioural scientists have asked is: what factors lead to the development of entrepreneurship? Researchers in western countries have revealed the following:

1. Society's values and needs: One value is crucial, saving the needs are of course for products and services which increase human welfare in society.
2. Government: Government as a political institution has role to play to enact legislations and policies which give encouragement to entrepreneurs. Support for research on entrepreneurship in Nigeria would serve the same purpose. In some countries, e.g. Japan, government establishes model factory organizations for people to learn entrepreneurship
3. The family: This has a role to play. The proof of hard work habits, value for independence, co-operation and other values can be formed in a family where love prevails.
4. The school: This is the several institutions responsible for providing basic and specialized technical education which an entrepreneur must

have.
5. Work organization: Here are created job opportunities to give the would-be entrepreneur to gain practical experience. Management practices should also create organization climate that encourage the breeding of entrepreneurship.

1.6 Implications of the Behavioural Analysis

An interesting point of behaviour is that every living organism behaves, and therefore "knows" the facts. But some people may not be aware. Perhaps the psychological analyses will help to make the people factors aware of their roles in the development of entrepreneurship in Nigeria.

It must be emphasized that behavioural scientists conceive entrepreneurship as made up of three components.

i) The entrepreneur
ii) The enterprise organization which he/she creates.
iii) The result of the created activity in more, better and cheaper products and services for the wealth and welfare of the nation.

1.7 How does one become an Entrepreneur?

There are no rigid steps to take to become an entrepreneur. However the process can be conceptualized into six steps, but they do help to understand the process.

(1) Dissatisfaction with the Status-Quo: This may be paid employment, unemployment, under-employment, sudden retrenchment, poor salary, to mention a few.

(2) Determination and decision to do something about "a" above: Find another job, goes on one's own, that is, be self-employed and so on and so forth.

(3) Searching for what to do: This may be by replicating former employer's business, start a complete new business that no one has ventured into, list all possible areas of venture or do a trial and error of various businesses and select one.

(4) Research the market: To assess the viability of alternatives selected from "c" above, involves cost of production, finances, marketing and sales, competition, government policy and profitability.

(5) Implementation of decision: This includes:

i. Form a company or register the business name (sole proprietorship), decides whether the business is limited liability or partnership.

ii. Raise capital: means of raising capital depends on the form of business or company. Capital can be raised privately by directly appealing to potential investors, or publicly through sales of shares.

iii. Setting up the plant: this may include procure and install plant machinery and equipment, secure raw materials, personnel and test run. Set up the organizational structure of the company.

(6) Management of the business: When the business is in operation, there is need to ensure its proper management. Competent professionals have to be employed to take charge of the various functional areas of the business, which include; finance marketing, production, personnel and technical maintenance. For small companies some of these functions may be carried out by part-time staff as they may not have enough to justify employing on full-time basis. Alternatively, one professional may combine two or more functional areas.

CHAPTER TWO: ENTREPRENEURSHIP IN THEORY AND FRACTURE

2.1 What is a theory?

A theory according to the dictionary.com (2013) is a coherent group of tested general positions, commonly regarded as correct, that can be used as principles of explanation and prediction for a class of phenomenon. It can also be defined as a proposed explanation whose status is still conjectural and subject to experimentation, in contrast to well-established propositions that are regarded as reporting matters of actual fact. It is also a particular conception or view of something to be done or of the method of doing it. Systems of rules or principles:

2.2 Theories of Entrepreneurship and Entrepreneurial Motivation

These theories would be examined from economical,

sociological and psychological point of views.

2.3 Economic Theory
The economic theory of entrepreneurship maintains that:-
1. Entrepreneurship and economic growth take place when the economic conditions are favourable;
2. Economic incentives are the main motivation for entrepreneurial activities;
3. Economic incentives include taxation policy, industrial policy, sources of finance and raw materials, infrastructural availability, investment and market opportunities, access to information about market conditions, technology, etc.

2.4 Sociological Theory
Sociological theory emphasizes that:-
1. Entrepreneurship is likely to get a boost in a particular social culture.
2. Societal values, religious beliefs, customs, taboos influence the behaviour of individuals in a society.
3. The entrepreneur is a role performer according to the role expectations by the society.

2.5 Psychological Theory

Psychological theory emphasizes that:-

1. Entrepreneurship gets a boast when society has sufficient supply of individuals with necessary psychological characteristics.
2. The psychological characteristics include need for high achievement, a vision of foresight, ability to face opposition.
3. These characteristics are formed during the individual's upbringing which stress on standard of excellence, self-reliance and low father dominance.

2.6 Entrepreneurship Innovation Theory

This theory was propounded by Joseph Schumpeter who believes that entrepreneurship helps the process of development in an economy. According to him, an entrepreneur is the one who is innovated, creative and has a foresight. He stressed further that innovation occurs when the entrepreneur:

1. Introduces a new product
2. Introduces a new production method
3. Opens up a new market
4. Finds out a new organization in any industry
5. Finds out a new source of raw material supply
6. Introduces new organization in any industry.

The theory emphasizes on innovation, ignoring the risk taking and organizing abilities in an entrepreneur. According to Schumpeter, an entrepreneur is a large scale business man, who is rarely found in developing countries, where entrepreneurs are small scale businessmen who need to imitate rather than innovate.

2.7 Theory of High Achievement/Theory of Achievement Motivation

Mcclelland identified two characteristics of entrepreneurship:
1. Doing things in a new way and better way.
2. Decision making under uncertainty. He stressed that people with high achievement orientation (need to succeed) were more likely to become entrepreneurs. Such people are not influenced by money or external motives.

They consider profit to be a measure of success and competency.

2.8 Motivation Theory by Mcclelland (acquired needs theory)

According to McClelland, a person has three types of needs at any given time, which are:-

a.) Need for achievement (get success with one's own effort)
b.) Need for power (to dominate, influence others)
c.) Need for affiliation (maintain friendly relationship with others)

The need for achievement is the highest for entrepreneurs.

2.9 The Rakinada Experiment

This experiment was concluded by Mcclelland in America, Mexico and numbia.

Under this experiment, young adults were selected and put through a 3-month training programme. The training aimed at inducing the achievement motivation. The course content was:

1. Trainees were asked to control their thinking and talk to themselves positively.
2. They imagined themselves in need of challenges and success for which they had to set planned and achievable goals.
3. They strived to get concrete and frequent feedback.
4. They strive to imitate their role models/those who perform well.

2.10 Conclusion of the Experiment

1. Traditional beliefs do not inhibit an entrepreneur.
2. Sustainable training can provide necessary motivation to an entrepreneur.
3. The achievement motivation had a positive impact on the performance of the participants.

It was the Rakinada experiment that made people realize the importance of EDP (Entrepreneur Development Programme) to induce motivation and competence in young prospective entrepreneur.

CHAPTER THREE: OPPORTUNITY

3.1 Definition

Opportunity may be defined as a chance to become something better than one is currently is. It can also be seen as a chance to do something or an occasion when it is easy for you to do something (e.g. a chance to get a job, a chance to get married, a chance to travel abroad and so on and so forth). It is a common saying among people that: opportunity comes but once in life time, and when one opportunity is not taken or misused, one may not come across it again for life.

It is factual that there is high rate of unemployment in

Nigeria but, it is also very pertinent to say that business opportunities abound everywhere in Nigeria, some of these opportunities are yet to be taken by our unemployed graduates perhaps:

a. There is problem of finance;
b. People are afraid to take risk;
c. Inability to recognize good business opportunities;
d. Cumbersome protocol of obtaining loan from Nigeria financial institutions;
e. High interest rate;
f. Fear of the unknown;
g. Lack of collateral security;
h. Unstable business environment;
i. Mentality of looking for office job only after graduation; and
j. Infrastructural problems.

To buttress the above points is the fact that Nigeria has a large reserve of natural resources (oil, gas, solid minerals etc.) and an expansive untapped potential in agriculture, also Nigeria is clearly a huge market, offering immense opportunities for business. Though there are infrastructural problems but the spirit of entrepreneurship does not surrender to challenges. Many of these problems present opportunities for profitable business.

3.2 Requirements to Spot Viable Business Opportunities in Nigeria

a. Desire and commitment: To be able to see

opportunities that exist or are emerging, you must have a burning desire to start a business. It is the intensity of your desire that will open your eyes to the opportunities around you without a consuming passion, nothing serious can really be achieved.

b. Focus attention to the environment: You need to define and narrow down your interest, for more effectiveness. A narrower berth sharpens your instinct on your define areas of interest. It helps plant this interest deeply in your subconscious. That way, your goal remains on the top burner and emerging opportunities can hardly escape your attention.

c. Readiness to take action: Opportunities arise all the time. The problem is that we are often not ready for them and so fail to take action. When you mean business, you must put yourself in the right position to take action. See an advertised invitation to a business opportunity briefing in your area of interest, why not check it out by attending? If you are not impressed, you burst it and wait for something else.

d. Readiness to do any work: It is wrong to look down on certain jobs that either they are dirty, downgrading, do not befit a graduate, etc. one important fact is that you must be able to do something at anytime. An idle hand people say is the devil's workshop. When you are yet to get what you want, you must be ready to take what you get. There is no shame in doing a dirty job, what actually carries shame is the act of not doing any work. It is a popular saying among the Ijebu people that "money realized from packing faeces does not smell".

3.3 The Face of Business Opportunities

A business must have good patronage to be successful. The target market will only patronize your product or services if it meets a yearning need. In looking for a business opportunity, you need to identify a need-gap and fill it. Your potential for success is dependent on this relationship between a need and the solution you offer. The more intense the need and more appropriate your solution is, the more successful your business will be. So, look for business opportunities in the daily needs, pains, difficulties and desire of the people. Find a good solution at the right price for any of these and be sure you will soon be smiling to the bank.

The people's requirements also change over time, propelled by various factors. Your ability to see emerging trends may also be the key to a successful business. What works today may not be adequate or in tomorrow. You may find your opportunity by seeing where the shifts are leading.

3.4 Drivers of Opportunity

Paying attention to the following drivers of opportunities will help you when seeking out emerging business opportunities:

i. Government policy: Government remains the dominant player in our economy. Changes in government policy represent one major creator of business opportunities or the reverse. The ban of the importation of processed fruit drinks has unleashed a new wave of local fruit juice manufacturers; port concessions set some investors up for good money. The key is to analyze policies for inherent opportunities. Better still get to know about these policies while they are still on the fire. If you do a serious exercise today, you will identify a handful of impending policies that will generate life-changing opportunities.

ii. Technological changes: Watch out too for opportunities thrown up by changes in technology. Didn't many small and medium operators (mast-builders, sellers of phones and accessories, hawkers, etc.) harvest a fortune from the introduction of GSM technology in Nigeria? If you missed out, the good news is that new opportunities arise all the time. Just keep scanning and remain prepared.

iii. Natural resources: The country is rich in natural resources, some of which are yet to be exploited. These resources range from extractive to agricultural and other endowments. While huge exploitation costs may be involved in some cases, there are areas where small business can play effectively.

iv. Demographics: Analyzing the population profile and emerging trends provides a good guide to business opportunities. Who would not know that property development in Lagos and Abuja, for instance, will remain a profitable business for some time to come, given the rate of population growth of these cities? Think of the different segments of the population and their needs, changing tastes, emerging influences. These are pointers to where

business opportunities lie.
v. Public utilities: The weakness of your public utilities creates a huge demand-supply gap, leaving a yawning market to be serviced. Pure water production has done well as a business option because of the unmet demand for portable water. Sale of power-generating sets, inverters, UPS/stabilizers and various power devices has left many bank accounts in deep black. The failure of the public educational system has created successful entrepreneurs operating private educational institutions. More opportunities are still there, if only you look more closely.

3.5 Failures of Existing Companies and Businesses

Each time you are dissatisfied with the product, services or any feature of existing businesses, it may be a pointer to a business idea. Sometimes, you don't need to re-invent the wheel. You may not have to create a new product or service idea. Simply improving on what is currently provided may be all you require to succeed. Look out for what is available today that you can improve on product enhancement, better delivery experience for customers or whatsoever.

3.6 What to Consider When You Weigh the Options

In evaluating the options you identify, your goal is to

choose a business that inherently has good potentials of success. While the ultimate performance will depend on how well you run your business, starting on a strong footing will be important. Give careful consideration to the nature of the product or service. The following factors are important:

Consumables are products that are consumed and replaced. They offer a better guarantee of sustained demand, durable products, on the other hand, will be demanded less frequently. On a low working capital, you probably will prefer a product that moves fast and consumables will be your best belt.

Essentials are basic requirements which individual and households purchase all the time. Food items, toiletries, clothing, etc. fall into this category. A business rooted in these goods will, on balance stand on a stronger demand base than one that deals on luxury items. For a small beginner, these items are a safer bet.

Seasonality refers to consumption cycle which peaks at certain periods but may be flat or depressed at others. Umbrella sell well during the raining season but may not be in mush demand in the dry season. Unless handled with other product lines, such goods can create a cash flow nightmare in the off season. Consider a product that keeps you in business all year round.

3.7 Where to look

To ensure you pick up information on developments that can point you to evolving or existing opportunities, you need to make a habit of amassing these resources:

The media, publications that is print, electronic, etc. catching the news headlines in newspapers, magazines, radio, T.V, internet etc. should be and a usual habit. The internet, which has become a huge library, is a rich source of information. It is currency, extensive coverage and extraordinary accessibility makes it a choice source to use.

Government's policy documents, official statements, budgets, publications of the Central Bank, government agencies, business groups and researchers will keep you informed of important economic and public policy trusts. Opinions of experts, friends, family and public discussants can also direct attention to where things are happening.

In summary, starting a business is serious business and requires some serious work. Take some time to do some analysis based on the indicators outlined above. Chances are good that you will find an opportunity that suits you and forms a basis for your dream business opportunities in Nigeria.

CHAPTER FOUR: FORMS OF BUSINESS

4.1 Sole Proprietorship

The vast of small businesses start out as sole proprietorships. These firms are owned by one person usually the individual who has day-to-day responsibility for running and managing the business. Sole proprietorships own all the assets of the business and the profits generated by it. They also assume complete responsibility for any of its liabilities or debts. This type of business does not require large capital to start, that is, with as little as ₦5,000:00 one can begin or start Sole proprietorship. For example, with ₦5,000:00 one can do table water business or start petty trade.

4.2 Advantages of Sole Proprietorship
1. Easiest and least expensive form of business to organize.
2. The owner takes all the profit.
3. The owner is not required by the law to submit the audited balance sheet to the registrar of companies.
4. The business can easily be discontinued by the owner if he feels like doing so.
5. The owner only pay personal tax not company tax.
6. Quick decision is made possible
7. Commitment to make the business succeed is very high.

4.3 Disadvantages of Sole Proprietorship
1. Sole proprietorship has limited liability and are legally responsible for all debts against the business.
2. Limited capital: the owner may not be able to raise much capital as done by partnership.
3. The death of the owner may bring the business to an end.
4. In case the business fails, the proprietor may lose all his belongings.
5. Due to limited capital, he may not be able to employ the services of high calibre staff.

4.4 Partnership

Partnership is a form of business in which two or more people share ownership of a single business. The partners always have a legal agreement that stipulates how decisions will be made, profit will be shared, disputes will be resolved, how future partners will be admitted to the partnership, how partners can be bought out, or what steps will be taken to dissolve the partnership when needed.

When deciding how the partners would make profit, issue of crises, break-up area also taken into consideration and decided. This is because, many partnerships split up at crises times and unless there is a defined process, there will be even greater problems. The amount of capital each will contribute must also be decided.

4.5 Advantages of Partnership

1. If the business failed, the liability of the partners could be limited to what they have contributed to the business.
2. The partners have ability to raise fund than sole proprietor.
3. Profit from the business go to the partners
4. Capable employee may be allowed to the business if given incentive to become a partner
5. Skills of partners are directed towards the success of the business
6. It is easy to establish, however, time is needed to develop partnership agreement.

4.6 Disadvantages of Partnership

1. Partners are jointly and individually liable for the actions of other partners.
2. Disagreement often occurs as decisions are shared.
3. Profits are jointly shared.
4. The withdrawal or death of a partner sometimes may end the partnership if not properly handled.
5. The disloyalty of a partner may affect the profit of the business as every partners goes about transacting business on behalf of other members.

4.7 Types of Partnership

According to Obasan (2001) partners may be classified on the basis of liability, degree of management participation, share in the profit and the amount contributed by members to the business. Obasan stressed further that types of partners include:

i. General partners;
ii. Limited partners;
iii. Silent partners;
iv. Secret partners;
v. Sleeping or dormant partners;
vi. Nominal partners;
vii. Senior and junior partners.

1. General partners: These are owners of the business, they have the right to determine the actions of the partnership and are active in the management and control of the organization, and they are the partners with unlimited liability.

2. Limited partners: These are partners who only contributed to the partnership and are not participating in the management. They receive return on their investment however; they are not legally liable for the debt of the partnership.
3. Silent partners: These types of partners do not participate in the management of the business, though they may be known to the public as the owners. Examples are banks that contributed to a business but are not participating in the management of the business.
4. Secret partners: These are partners who participate in the management of the business but are not known to the public.
5. Sleeping or dormant partners: These are partners who share from the profit/loss of the business but do not participate in the business, also they are not known to the public. Their profit/loss depends on the amount contributed to the business.
6. Nominal partners: These are those who publicize to the public that they are partners although they have no investment in the business and therefore have no right to participate in management. They only lend their names to the enterprise and may be liable for the debt of the organization.
7. Senior and junior partners: Senior partners are partners, who has large investment in the enterprise and also, participate effectively in the management of the enterprise as a result of years of experience. While junior partners have no investment in the business, and are newly admitted. They do not play any key role in the management of the business.

4.8 Corporation

This is an association of individuals, created by law or under authority of law, having a continuous existence independent of the existence of its members, and powers and liabilities distinct from those of its members (dictionary.com 2013). The word "corporation" derives from corpus, the Latin word for body, or "a body of people" by the time of Justinian, Roman law recognized a range of corporate entities under the names universitas, corpus.

Corporation can also be defined as a legal entity that has been incorporated through a legislative or registration process established through legislation. Incorporated entities have legal rights and liabilities that are distinct from their employment and shareholders, and may conduct business as either a profit seeking business or not for profit business.

Early incorporated entities were established by Charter (i.e. by Adhoc Act granted by a monarch or passed by a parliament or legislature.) most jurisdictions now allow the creation of new compositions through registration. In addition to legal personality, registered companies tend to have limited liability, be owned by shareholders who can transfer the shares to others, and controlled by a board of directors whom the shareholders appoint (Wikipedia.org, 1913).

4.9 Advantages of Corporation
1. Shareholders would only loose what they contributed to the business in case the business liquidates.
2. Corporation can raise additional funds through the sale of stock.
3. It has access to large sum of capital.
4. It makes more profits if properly managed.
5. It may deduct the cost of benefits it provides to officers and employees.
6. The company can be taxed similarly to a partnership if it elects corporation status and meet the requirements.

4.10 Disadvantages of Corporation
1. The process of incorporation is very cumbersome and requires more time and money than any other forms of organizations.
2. Corporations are monitored and control by federal, state and some local agencies, thus, may have more paper work to comply with.
3. Incorporating may result in higher overall taxes, also dividends paid to shareholders cannot be deducted from business income, this may result to taxing the income twice.

A tax election only: This election enables the shareholder to treat the earnings and profits as distributions, and have them pass through directly to their personal tax return. The catch here is that the shareholder, if working for the company, and if there is a profit, must pay his/herself wages, and it must standard of reasonable compensation. This can vary by geographical region as well as occupation, but the basic rule is to pay yourself what you will have to pay someone to do your job, as long as there is enough profit. If you do not do this, the internal revenue service can reclassify all of the earnings and profit as wages, and you will be liable for all of the payroll taxes on the total amount.

4.11 Cooperative Society

A cooperative society is an autonomous association of persons who voluntarily cooperate for their mutual, social, economic and cultural benefit. Cooperatives include non profit community organizations and businesses that are owned and managed by the people who use its services (a consumer cooperative) or by the people who work there (a worker cooperative) or by the people who live there (a housing cooperatives) that are also consumer cooperative societies or credit unions, multi stakeholder cooperative such as those that brings together civil society and local unions to deliver community needs, and third tier cooperatives whose members are cooperatives.

Membership of a cooperative society is voluntary, everyone is free to join or leave the society as he wishes. Management of the society is based on the principle of democracy, that is, one man one vote during the annual general meeting (AGM) or when taking vital decisions that require voting. Unlike the situation with the cooperation where members, exercise their franchise on the basis of their investments, with cooperative societies, no matter the amount the individuals have contributed, no one has double chances, that is, all members are equal.

Some of the commonest cooperative societies are the thrift and credit societies, agricultural cooperatives, consumer cooperatives and artisan societies. Cooperative principles are the roles and regulations governing the cooperative societies. These are referred to as Rochdale principles in honour of the investor of these principles. They include:

1. Open or voluntary members i.e. freedom to join and leave the organization as long as he meets the required qualifications.
2. Democracy: Voting on the basis of one man one vote, this differs from corporation's policy of one

share one vote.

3. Limited interest on capital: The capital invested by each member attracts limited interest

4. Patronage rebates: This refers to payment of dividend on the basis of the amount contributed and patronage made by each member. This may be the magnitude to which each member has utilized the services provided by the organization. For example, in thrift and credit cooperative societies, the more loan you obtain from the society, the better your dividend. Dividends are paid on the amount you contributed to the society and the loan obtained.

5. Cash sales: In most cases, all transactions are done on cash and carry basis. But sometimes, members are granted credit purchases with interest to be paid to the society.

6. Cooperative education: They educate the members and non members regularly on good business opportunities that would earn or can earn them good dividend. Sometimes they trade with member's capital in order to make profit.

7. Cooperation among co-operators.

8. Neutrality in ethnic, race, religion, education and politics.

CHAPTER FIVE: STAFFING

5.1 Introduction

The term staffing in management consists of:
1. Selecting the right person for the right post.
2. Training and development.
3. Giving proper remuneration and motivation.
4. Performance appraisal of employees.
5. Proper promotions, transfers, etc.

Staffing means filling and keeping filled, positions in the organization structure. Before staffing is embarked upon, the entrepreneur must have decided the category of staff needed for the business, their qualifications, salaries and schedule of duties. When one is starting a small scale business, he does not need a large number of staff, for example, a staff can serve a dual purpose e.g. an accountant can also double as the sales clerk. This system is necessary to cut down cost.

There are some internal and external factors affecting staffing and these include:

5.2 Internal Factors Affecting Staffing

1. Promotion policy: Staffing is affected by the promotion policy of the organization. If the organization has a good promotion policy with prospects to career growth and development, only then efficient people will be attracted to the organization. Internal promotion is better and necessary for lower and middle-level jobs. This is because it increases the morale and motivation of the staff. However, for top level jobs, the "right" person may be from within the organization, or

he/she may be selected from outside.

2. Future growth plans: Staffing is also affected by the future growth plans of the organization. If the organization wants to grow and expand then it will need many talented people. in order to grow and expand, the organization must select experts and give them continuous training and development.

3. Technology used: Staffing is also affected by the technology used by the organization. If the organization uses modern technologies, then it must have continuous training programs to update the technical knowledge of their staff.

4. Support from top management: Staffing is also affected by the support from top management. If the top management gives full support to it then the organization can have scientific selection procedures, scientific promotion and transfer policies, continuous development programs, career development programs, etc.

5. Image of organization: Staffing is also affected by image of the organization in the job market. If it has a good image then staffing will attract the best employees and managers. An organization earns a good image only if it maintains good policies and practices. This includes job security, training and

development, promotion, good working environment, work culture and so on and so forth.

5.2 External Factors Affecting Staffing

1. Labour laws: Labour laws of the government also affect the staffing policy of the organization. For example, the organization has to support 'social equality and upliftment policies of the government by giving job reservations to candidates coming from depressed classes like Scheduled Castes (SC), Scheduled Tribes (ST), Other Backward Classes (OBC), etc. and even to those who are physically handicapped (PH). It is mandatory for an organization not to recruit children in their workforce and stop child labour. The provision of 'Minimum Wages Act' guides an organization to fix minimum salaries of employees and stop their economic exploitation.

2. Pressure from socio-political groups: Staffing is also affected by activities of socio-political groups and parties. These group and parties put pressure on the organization to grant jobs only to local people. The concept of "sons of soil" is becoming popular in India, and even Nigeria.

3. Competition: In India, there is a large demand for

high qualified and experienced staff. This has resulted in competition between different organizations to attract and hire efficient staffing policies, offer attractive salaries and other job benefits in order to add the best minds in their workforce.

4. Educational standards: Staffing is also affected by the educational standard of an area. If the educational standard of a place is very high then the organization will only select qualified and experienced staff for all job positions. For example, some I.T. company in India, only prefer skilled candidates with computer or I.T. engineering degree for the post of software developer.

5. Other external factors: Staffing is also affected by other external factors such as trade unions, social attitude towards work, etc.

5.3 How to Get Quality Staff into Your Business

The entrepreneur cannot do it alone. He needs staff to handle the various segments of production and distribution of goods and services. Though the number of staff required is determined by the type and nature of the business, however, what is certain here is that staff must be employed to handle certain areas. As an entrepreneur one needs to opt for the best within the limited available resources. There are ways by which an entrepreneur can get high calibre staff recruited into his business. These include:

1. Advertisement: This is done by advertisement in the news paper, production of posters/handbills and posting of such in strategic places or in television. Newspaper and television advertisement are very effective but costly. It enables the entrepreneur to select competent staff by means of personal interview. As earlier said, most small scale business owners may not be able to use newspaper/television advertisement because of the cost.

2. Employment agency: An entrepreneur may contract employment agency for recruitment of their staff. The employment agent would now advertise for the needed staff, interview and recruit for their client. The employment agent charges their client for the services rendered. This means of recruitment is also good but not the best as the agent may be biased and recruit their family and associates instead of the most competent and qualified candidates.

3. Educational institutions: An entrepreneur aspiring for the best staff for his business can visit higher institution turning out graduates to place an order for the recruitment of graduates with the best

results. Business owners made use of this medium very well in the past. It is one of the best ways to secure quality staff into one's business if only one has the resources to meet the cost because the best graduates would like to collect the best salaries.

4. Labour office: One can get his staff through labour office, but the staff gotten through this means may not be the best because only applicants who have tried various places without success result to labour offices.

5. Churches/mosques: Announcement for staff vacancy can be made in the church/mosque. It is believed that staff recruited through this medium would be dedicated, committed and loyal to their employers. However, experience have showed that this is not always true, sometimes those recruited from religious houses prove to be more worldly than those recruited from other sources.

6. Committed and dedicated staff: A Staff that is very hardworking and committed to his work may be asked to bring his friend. The rationale behind this is that a hardworking person would have a hardworking friend. In most cases this has proved to be true.

7. National Youth Service Corps (NYSC): NYSC

office may be contacted to provide dedicated corps member for employment after service. Employers make use of this medium regularly. It is one of the best and it does not cost anything to the employer.

8. Radio advertisement: This is another medium of getting quality staff into one's business. Radio covers a large area of the country; it enables applicants from far and wide to respond to such advertisement. Thus, employer/entrepreneur would be able to select the best candidates. It is also costly to use this medium.

9. Chalk/signboard: Vacancy may be written on chalk/signboard and be placed in strategic places. Some small scale business owners often made use of this means. However, this medium is not the best as the respondents can only come from the local environment, not wide enough to attract applicants from other parts of the city or state.

10. Mouth to mouth: An entrepreneur may inform friends, relations, club members who are also entrepreneurs or employers of labour to help in bringing committed and employable staff. In most cases, this medium would also lead to the employment of capable hands as the friends, relations and clubs members would only introduce

applicants that they can trust, who would not tarnish their reputations.

CHAPTER SIX: MANAGEMENT AND ADMINISTRATION OF SMALL AND MEDIUM SCALE BUSINESSES

6.1 Introduction

However defined, small and medium enterprises are so important few if any part of our economy could go on without them, without their products, a never failing supply potential entrepreneur who is ready to take business risks by exploiting new ideas or perceive favourable market opportunities. They provide career opportunities and provide excellent outlets of the energy of those who prefer to work-and are happiest and most productive in the structure and environment of a small-medium enterprises. It has been recognized that in many industries, small and medium enterprises can respond more quickly and at less cost than big business to the quickening rate of change in products processes, services and markets. Small and medium business enjoys infinite variety of choice of goods and services. For the mass market as their main target, smaller firms strive to serve the need and interest of defined customers. Small and medium enterprises are believed to create more jobs per unit of invested capital and per units of energy consumed. They help a great deal to spread modern technology all over the nooks and crannies of the country.

Among other benefits derived from small scale enterprises as reiterated by Oladele (1988), are that they tend to check urban/rural migration, help to conserve foreign exchange and promote the development of indigenous entrepreneurial skills. They handle special and varied products which the large firms do not specialized in and provide training on the post or on the job. Besides, small businesses contribute to the national output, help in the dispersal of industries and the growth in the quality of life of rural areas where they mostly operate.

Obikoya (1995) observes that small-medium business can serve as instruments for individual development. Their dependence on traditional skills can contribute to building up of the supply of managerial, manufacturing and entrepreneurship experience, which in turn can form the basis for industrial expansion. Furthermore, small/medium business economizes with the scarce factors of producing the kind of consumer goods which the domestic market can acquire and is more likely to be affordable.

Small-medium enterprises often serve as the basic grounds for new ideas and products, patented or unpatented. Though many of these may never achieve public acceptance, but they must be given a trial before it is possible to know their future. Big business tends to be conservative in this respect and some of our cherished consumers products would still be in the scientific fiction stage, but for the clearing pioneer efforts of small and medium business owners with confidence in new ideas and creativity.

If means are adopted to encourage their modernization and growth in provincial areas and semi-rural areas, they may tap hitherto unused resources in the form of workers who are unemployed or employed only in certain seasons. Small and medium enterprises are also able to resist the show balling and overhead costs that plague many large concerns. Flexibility and adaptability are virtues of small and medium business, contracting sharply with cumbersome procedure of large organizations.

Oyedijo (1991), contends that small and medium enterprises spark the economic through their creative activities and make for a more balance economic development. Initiation of structural, innovation and creative economic are easy to come by with small and medium scales industries without forcing a large part of the population out of work. They give reward broader and more significant to the concept of Nigerianization of the economy. They ensure that Nigerians have a strong hold on their economy, this bringing about real economic and political power and beverage.

6.2 The Future of Business and Succession Issue

Sooner or later, everyone wants to retire. But if you own a family business (foremost small businesses are family business) retirement isn't just a matter of deciding not to go to office any more. Besides ensuring that you have enough money to retire on, the whole question of what happens to the business when you're no longer running it becomes paramount. Who's going to manage the business when you no longer work the business? How will ownership be transferred? Will your business even carry on or will you sell it?

Succession planning seeks to manage these issues, setting up a smooth transition between you and the future owners of your business. With family business, succession planning can be especially complicated because of the relationship and emotions involved and because most people are not that comfortable discussing topics such as ageing, death and their financial affairs.

But comfortable or not, succession planning should be a priority for any family business.

More than 70% of family-owned businesses do not survive the transition from founder to second generation. In most cases, the "killer" is taxes or family discord, both issues that a good family business succession plan will cover.

Think of business succession planning as broken into the three main issues; management, ownership, and taxes. It's important to realize that management and ownership are not necessary one and the same. You may decide, for instance, to transfer management of your business to just one of your children, whether they're actively involved in operating the business or not.

The taxes component of succession planning looks at the minimization of taxes upon death. There are assets transfer tax strategies that will help you do this, such as freezing the value of interest in the company while you transfer ownership to your children. Accountants and lawyers who specialize in succession planning can provide invaluable advice about tax strategies.

For many family businesses, family is the primary emphasis of succession planning. Whether you're thinking about future management of your business, how ownership is going to be passed along, or taxes, you won't be able to help thinking about how decisions will affect your family.
What can you do to make succession planning less painful and more successful for your family business? Use this tips for family business succession planning to get the succession planning process underway and ensure a smoother transition from one generation to another.

i. Start succession planning early. Five years in advance is good. Ten years in advance is better. Many business advisors tell budding entrepreneurs to build an exit strategy right into their business plan. The point is the longer you get to spend on family business succession planning; the smoother the transition process is likely to be.

ii. Involve your family in business succession planning discussion. Making your own succession plan and then announcing it, is the surest way to sow family discord. Opening a dialogue among family members is the best way to begin the process of a successful succession plan-one where attention is paid to the personal feelings, ambitions and goals of everyone concerned.

iii. Look at your family realistically and plan accordingly. You may want your first-born son to run the business, but does he have the business skills or even the interest to do it? Perhaps there's another family member who is more capable. It may even be that there are no family members capable or interested in continuity of the business and that, it would be best to sell it. Examine the strengths of all possible successors as objectively as possible and think about what's best for the business.

iv. Get over the idea that everyone has to have an equal share. While this is a nice idea in theory, it may not be in the best interest of your business. Remember that management and ownership are separate business succession planning issues. It may be fairer for the successor (s) you have chosen to run the business to have a larger share of business ownership than family members not active in the business. Or it may be best to transfer both management and ownership to your chosen successor and make other financial arrangements to benefits your other children.

v. Train your successor (s) and work with them. How can you expect your successor to take over and run your business successfully if you haven't spent any time training him or her? Your family business succession plan will have a much better chance of success if you work with your successor (s) for a year or two before you hand over the batton. For entrepreneurs, sharing decision making and teaching business skills to someone else can be difficult, but it's definitely an effort that will pay big dividends for the business.

vi. Get outside help with your succession planning. Lawyers, accountants, financial advisors, there are many professionals that can help you put together a successful succession plan. There are even companies that specialized in family business succession planning; who will facilitates the process of working throughout both family and succession plan issues.

If you want to pass your family business along to the next generation, putting off succession planning is the worst thing you can do. A good succession plan can ensure that you have the funds you need to retire and that the business you have built continues to thrive.

CHAPTER SEVEN: MARKETING AND MARKETING SEGMENT

7.1 Introduction

Marketing is concerned with all stages of operation which aid the movement of commodities from the productions site to the consumers, and these include assemblage of goods, storage, transportation, processing, grading and financing of all these activities. (Adegeye and Ditto, 1982).

7.2 The Functions of Marketing

It is generally accepted that with respect to business/organization, marketing involves five main functions, namely:

1. Market research (into needs/wants, the environment etc.)
2. Producing the correct products;
3. Promoting the product;
4. Distributing the product } Marketing Mix
5. Pricing the product

To be noted is that the later four are usually grouped together as the marketing mix. The marketing mix is the set of controllable variables which is selected by a market in order to achieve certain predetermined objectives.

7.3 The Objectives of Marketing

1. **Increase sales:** No business can survive without ensuring an adequate level of sales in order to cover its cost and provide an element of profit for the entrepreneur. Most entrepreneurs are driven by profit maximization motive, and such all entrepreneurs are constantly seeking to increase their level of sales.

2. **Increase market share:** The level of market share held by an entrepreneur is an important driven force. It has been opined that a business can only compete successfully in market in which they are the market leaders. Actually this may not be true in some instances; otherwise all market structures would rapidly become monopolized. Quite often in competitive market, the objectives may be to simply maintain the level of market share currently held by the business. Another way of illustrating this is under condition of competitive oligopoly. The competitors may all be reasonably satisfied with their level of market share, until one undertakes an aggressive marketing campaign to boost penetration, for example, by a reduction in price. Almost inevitably, this will result in retaliatory

action by the rest of the market, and market share levels will generally return to their pre-competitive state, but all business will be left with profit levels.

3. **Enhancement of product:** On many occasions, marketing activities are undertaken not simply to increase immediate level of sales but in order to enhance the image of the product in the eye of the consumer. This is frequently done using various promotional tools. In the past, Guinness Stout sponsored some of the very successful TV action movies titled "Michael Power", as a result, the level of awareness and consumer perception of its product rose substantially.

4. **Quality assurance:** This is another objective of marketing. It aims at reassuring consumers about the quality of a particular product. This can be done in a variety of ways, including the use of pricing and distribution policies.

7.4 Partial Analysis of the Marketing Mix: Product

It has been argued that product, which is the first element of marketing mix is the most important. A product of well designed and of high quality may sell itself, even in the absence of marketing communication and poor distribution network to support it. The opposite will happen to a wrong product even when all the supports are excellent.

7.5 Analyzing Products:

A product is basically anything, which an organization sells. The product does not have to be physical, it can also be service. The important is that people buy to satisfy needs.

There are four stages for analyzing product

1. **The generic product:** These are products without any packaging or branding attached. These days most products are branded. A good example of generic products is farm produce in Nigeria.
2. **The expected product:** When people buy a product, say a radio cassette player, they expect additional things from it, they include certain quality of sound stereo, wave band and sophisticated controls. These requirements are the expected product, and very quickly become the norm or generic product as such, any organization wishing to compete at even the lowest of markets must conform with these minimum expectation levels.

3. **The Augmented product:** In order to gain an advantage over their competitors, suppliers always try to offer something over and above the expected product. The augmentation may be physical, for instance, by the addition of new feature or use.
4. **The potential product:** The potential includes everything that might be done to attract and hold customers.

7.6 The product range

Products are continuously evolving to meet ever-changing market needs. The potential product becomes the augmented product, which in turn becomes the expected product. Companies that depend on one product are always in a vulnerable position in today's rapidly changing environment. For example, a five star hotel will offer not only accommodation but also leisure facilities, catering, banqueting, restaurants and bar facilities. As most industries are still growing and experiencing rapid change, the products within must be monitored and managed carefully to ensure that dying products are replaced with new ones at the appropriate times.

7.7 New product development

The process of new product development is inherent in all

organizations who are seeking continued success. It must be a continuous process, as products, market and consumers are all constantly changing. There are various stages through which all new products must go, and these are as follows:

i. Idea generation
ii. Screening
iii. Market analysis
iv. Product development
v. Product testing
vi. Commercialization/Launch

7.8 Idea generation

Numerous methods exist for the generation of new ideas. Ideas are basis of all new products. While some products are classified as 'Innovative', other new products are 'Adaptive'. Adaptive products are not classified as inventions but just modifications.

The first task of a business intention on an effective new product development programs is to create an atmosphere in which the communication of new ideas flourish. A number of specific techniques may be used to stimulate the generation of ideas, namely:

- Brainstorming
- Suggestion box

- Research and development
- The sales force

CHAPTER EIGHT: INSURANCE

8.1 Meaning of Insurance

Insurance is the equitable transfer of the risk of a loss from one entity to another in exchange for payment. It is a form of risk management primarily used to hedge against the risk of contingent, uncertain loss.

An insurer, or insurance carrier, is a company selling the insurance; the insured, or policy holder, is the person or entity buying the insurance policy. The amount of money to be charged for a certain amount of insurance coverage is called the premium. Risk management, the practice of appraising and controlling risk, has evolved as a discrete field of study and practice.

The transaction involves the insured assuming a guarantee and known relatively small loss in the form of payment to the insurer in exchange for the insurer's promise to compensate (indemnify) the insured in the case of financial (personal) loss. The insured receives a contract, called the insurance policy, which details the conditions and circumstances under which the insured will be financially compensated

8.2 What is Business Insurance?

"Business Insurance" is a broad name for different coverage available to the business owner to protect against losses and to insure the continuing operation of the business.

Most people are familiar with insurance for their personal home and automobile. This coverage protects you financially in case of an accident or disaster to your home or car. We are familiar with these types of insurance because it is natural for most people to realize that they would be unable to replace their home tomorrow if there was a fire or to replace their automobile if there was an accident.

The same principle applies to business insurance. The principle is one of risk. There are risks that, while they may never occur, are so destructive that it makes sense to plan ahead and manage the risk. In our personal lives these risks are often more easily foreseeable.

For our businesses however, we often do not consider risk or believe that the risk cannot be managed and so we turn a blind eye hoping that nothing 'bad' happens. Some businesses owners have worked with believe that since their business is profitable with a positive cash flow they can take care of the disaster when it happens. They forget that if the business is not operating - there is no cash flow.

Business insurance is nothing more than spreading and managing the risk among many business owners. Insurance companies take premium payments from many covered businesses, invest those payments, and create a pool of money to pay out to a covered business if that business has a covered loss. Over the last 300 years, insurers have developed mathematical models to determine what chance there is of a risk occurring and, in so doing, what premiums the insurer must charge to stay in business and make a profit. Over that same time, insurers have developed approximately eight to nine general categories of losses that seem to happen with more frequency. The insurers developed particular policies to address those types of losses.

Business insurance is a broad description that encompasses these different types of policies. Because there are so many different types of coverage it is confusing. But, at the very basic level, the concept is the same - the management of risk.

8.3 Preparing to Purchase Insurance

Managing the risk your company faces is a constant effort. But, the first step is preparing to purchase insurance. The following is an outline of that process that will prove helpful:

1. **Learn About Different Types of Coverage**

    Take time to develop an understanding of the types of coverage available in order to discuss then with your insurance professional. You may not need to know the intricacies of any particular coverage, but understanding, for example, that property insurance is necessary to protect a business location, it is a basic concept that goes a long way to making you an informed business owner.

2. **Analyze Your Business**

    Analyze you business to make an assessment of what coverage you will need now and make some educated guesses at what your business will need in the future. Sometimes the easiest way to do this is to speak with others in your industry. Prepare a description of your business that you have written out so you can quickly interview different insurance professionals in seeking quotes of coverage.

3. **Choose an Insurance Professional**

    Much like an accountant or lawyer, your insurance professional should be someone with whom you plan to develop an ongoing relationship. Choosing an insurance professional and working with that professional is made easier when you have a clear understanding of your business and its direction as well as a general idea of what types of policies are available.

4. **Review Your Initial Business Plan Regularly**

    At the initial purchase, set a calendared date to review your business insurance plan with your insurance professional regularly. Things change in business. Commit yourself to monitor that change and review the need for more or less coverage on a regular and continuing basis.

8.4 Principles

Insurance involves pooling funds from many insured entities (known as exposures) to pay for the losses that some may incur. The insured entities are therefore protected from risk for a fee, with the fee being dependent upon the frequency and severity of the event occurring. In order to be an insurable risk, the risk insured against must meet certain characteristics. Insurance as a financial intermediary is a commercial enterprise and a major part of the financial services industry, but individual entities can also self-insure through saving money for possible future losses (Gollier, 2003).

8.5 Insurability

Risk which can be insured by private companies typically shares seven common characteristics.

1. **Large number of similar exposure units**: Since insurance operates through pooling resources, the majority of insurance policies are provided for individual members of large classes, allowing insurers to benefit from the law of large numbers in which predicted losses are similar to the actual losses. Exception includes Lloyd's of London, which is famous for insuring the life or health of actors, sport figures, and other famous individuals. However, all exposures will have particular differences, which may lead to different premium rates.
2. **Definite loss**: The loss takes place at a known time, in a known place, and from a known cause. The classic example is death of an insured person on a life insurance policy, fire, automobile accidents, and

worker injuries may all meet this criterion. Other types of losses may only be definite in theory. Occupational disease, for instance, may involve prolonged exposure to injurious conditions where no specific time, place, or cause is identifiable. Ideally, the time, place and cause of a loss should be cleared enough that a reasonable person, with sufficient information, could objectively verify all three elements.

3. **Accidental loss**: The event that constitute the trigger of a claim should be fortuitous, or at least outside the control of the beneficiary of the insurance. The loss should be pure, in the sense that it results from an event for which there is only the opportunity for cost. Events that contain speculative elements, such as ordinary business risks or even purchasing a lottery ticket, are generally not considered insurable.

4. **Large loss**: The size of the loss must be meaningful from the perspective of the insured. Insurance premiums need to cover both the expected cost of losses, plus the cost issuing and administering the policy, adjusting losses, and supplying the capital needed to reasonably assure that the insurer will be able to pay claims. For small losses, these later

costs may be several times the size of the expected cost of losses. There is hardly any point in paying such costs unless the protection offered has real value of a buyer.

5. **Affordable premium**: If the likelihood of an insured event is so high, or the cost of event so large, that the resulting premium is large relative to the amount of protection offered, then it is not likely that the insurance will be purchased, even if on offer. Furthermore, as the accounting profession formally recognizes the financial accounting standards, the premium cannot be so large that there is not a reasonable chance of a significant loss to the insurer. If there is no such chance of loss, then the transaction may have the form of insurance, but not the substance.

6. **Calculable loss**: There are two elements that must be at least estimable, if not formally calculable: the probability of loss, and the attendant cost. Probability of loss is generally an empirical exercise, while cost has more to do with the ability of a reasonable person in possession of a copy of the insurance policy and a proof of loss associated with a claim presented under that policy to a reasonable definite and objective evaluation of the

amount of the loss recoverable as a result of the claim.

7. **Limited risk of catastrophically large losses**: Insurable losses are ideally independent and non-catastrophic, meaning that the losses do not happen all at once and individual losses are not severe enough to bankrupt the insurer; insurers may prefer to limit their exposure to a loss from a single event to some small portion of their capital base. Capital constraints insurer's ability to sell earthquake insurance as well as wind insurance in hurricane zones. In the US, flood risk is insured by the Federal Government. In commercial fire insurance, it is possible to find single properties whose total exposed value is well in excess of any individual insurer's capital constraint. Such properties are generally shared among several insurers, or are insured by single insurer whose syndicates the risk into the reinsurance market.

8.6 Legal

When a company insures an individual entity, there are basic legal requirements. Several commonly cited legal principles of insurance according to Irish Brokers Association (2009) include:

1. **Indemnity**: The insurance company indemnifies, or compensates, the insured in the case of certain losses only up to the insured's interest.

2. **Insurable interest**: The insured typically must directly suffer from the loss. Insurable interest must exist whether property insurance or insurance on a person is involved. The concept requires that the insured have a "stake" in the loss or damage to the life or property insured. What that "stake" is will be determined by the kind of insurance involved and the nature of the property ownership or relationship between the persons. The requirement of an insurable interest is what distinguishes insurance from gambling.

3. **Utmost good faith**: (Uberrima fides) the insured and the insurer are bound by a good faith bond of honesty and fairness. Material facts must be disclosed.

4. **Contribution**: Insurers which have similar obligations to the insured contribute in the indemnification, according to some methods.

5. **Subrogation**: The insurance company acquires legal rights to pursue recoveries on behalf of the insured, for example, the insurer may sue those liable for the insured's loss.

6. **Causal proximal, or proximate cause**: the cost of loss (the peril) must be covered under the insuring agreement of the policy, and the dominant cause must not be excluded.
7. **Mitigation**: In the case of any loss or casualty, the asset owner must attempt to keep loss to a minimum, as if the asset was not insured.

8.7 Indemnification

To "indemnify" means to make whole again, or to be reinstated to the position that one was in, to the extent possible, prior to the happening of a specified event or peril. Accordingly, life insurance is generally not considered to be indemnity insurance, but rather "contingent" insurance (i.e. a claim arises on the occurrence of a specified event). There are generally three types of insurance contracts that seek to indemnify an insured:

i. a "reimbursement" policy, and
ii. A "pay on behalf" or "on behalf of" policy, and
iii. An "indemnification" policy.

From an insured's standpoint, the result is usually the same: the insurer pays the loss and claims expenses.

If the insured has a "reimbursement" policy, the insured

can be required to pay for a loss and then be "reimbursed" by the insurance carrier for the loss and out of pocket costs including, with the permission of the insurer, claim expenses

Under a "pay on behalf" policy, the insurance carrier would defend and pay a claim on behalf of the insured that would not be out of pocket for anything. Most modern liability insurance is written on the basis of "pay on behalf" language which enables the insurance carrier to manage and control the claim.

Under an "indemnification" policy, the insurance carrier can generally either "reimburse" or "pay on behalf of", whichever is more beneficial to it and the insured in the claim handling process.

An entity seeking to transfer risk (an individual, corporation, or association of any type, etc) becomes the "insured" party once risk is assumed by an 'insurer', the issuing party, by means of a contract, called an insurance policy. Generally, an insurance contract includes, at a minimum, the following elements: identification of participating parties (the insurer, the insured, the beneficiaries), the premium, the period of coverage, the particular loss event covered, the amount of coverage (i.e.

the amount to be paid to the insured or beneficiary in event of a loss), and exclusions (event not covered). An insured is thus said to be "indemnified" against the loss covered in the policy.

When insured parties experience a loss for a specified peril, the coverage entities, the policy holder to make a claim against the insurer for the covered amount of loss as specified by the policy. The fee paid by the insured to the insurer for assuming the risk is called the premium. Insurance premiums from many insured are used to fund account reserved for later payment of claims - in theory for relatively few claimants - and for overhead costs. So long as an insurer maintains adequate funds set aside for anticipated losses (called reserves), the remaining margin is an insurer's profit

8.8 Societal Effects

Insurance can have various effects on society through the way that it changes who bears the cost of losses and damage. On one hand, it can increase fraud, on the other, it can help societies and individuals prepare for catastrophes and mitigate the effects of catastrophes on both households and societies.

Insurance can influence the probability of losses through moral hazard, insurance fraud, and preventive steps by the insurance company. Insurance scholars have typically used moral hazard to refer to the increased loss due to unintentional carelessness and moral hazard to refer to increase risk due to intentional carelessness or indifference (Dembe and Borden, 2000). Insurers attempt to address carelessness through inspections, policy provision requiring certain types of maintenance and possible discounts for loss mitigation efforts. While in theory insurers could encourage investment in loss reduction, some commentators have argued that in practice insurers had historically not aggressively pursued loss control measures - particularly to prevent disaster losses such as hurricanes - because of concerns over rate reductions and legal battles. However, since about 1996 insurers have begun to take a more active role in loss mitigation, such as through building codes (Kunreuther, 1996).

8.9 Insurers' Business Model

The business model is to collect more in premium and investment income than is paid out in losses, and to also offer a competitive price which consumers will accept.

Profit can be reduced to a simple equation:

Profit = earned premium + investment income - incurred loss - underwriting expenses.

Insurer makes money in two ways:

* Through underwriting, the process by which insurers select the risks to insure and decide how much in premium to charge for accepting those risks.
* By investing the premiums they collect from insured parties.

The most complicated aspect of the insurance business is the actuarial science of rate making (price setting) of policies, which uses statistics and probability to approximate the rate of future claims based on a given risk. After producing rates, the insurer will use discretion to reject or accept risks through the underwriting process.

At the most basic level, initial ratemaking involves looking at the frequency and severity of insured perils and the expected average payout resulting from these perils. Thereafter, an insurance company will collect historical loss data, bring the loss data to present value, and compare these prior losses to the premium collected in order to assess rate adequacy. Loss ratios and expense loads are also used. Rating for different risk characteristics involves at the most basic level comparing the losses with "loss relatives" - a policy with twice as many losses would therefore be charged twice as much. More complex multivariate analyses are sometimes used when multiple characteristics are involved and a univariate analysis could produce confounded results. Other statistical methods may be used in assessing the probability of future losses.

Upon termination of given policy, the amount of premium collected minus the amount paid out in claims is the insurance underwriting profit on that policy. Underwriting performance is measured by something called the combined ratio which is the ratio of expenses/losses to premiums. A combined ratio of less than 100% indicates an underwriting profit, while anything over 100 indicates an underwriting loss. A company with a combined ratio over 100% may nevertheless remain profitable due to investment earnings.

Insurance companies earn investment profits on "float". Float or available reserve, is the amount of money at hand at any given moment that an insurer has collected in insurance premiums but has not paid out in claims. Insurer start investing insurance premiums as soon as they are collected and continue to earn interest or other income on them until claims are paid out. The Association of British

Insurers (gathering 400 insurance companies and 94% of UK insurance services) has almost 20% of the investment in the London Stock Exchange.

In the United States, the underwriting loss of property and casualty insurance companies was $142.3 billion in the five years ending 2003. But overall profit for the same period was $68.4 billion, as the result of float. Some insurance industry insiders, most notably Hank Greenberg, do not believe that it is forever possible to sustain a profit from float without an underwriting profit as well, but this opinion is not universally held.

Naturally, the float method is difficult to carry out in an economically depressed period. Bear markets do cause insurers to shift away from investments and to toughen up their underwriting standards, so a poor economy generally means high insurance premiums. This tendency is swing between profitable and unprofitable periods over time are commonly known as the underwriting, or insurance cycle.

8.10 Claims

Claims and loss handling is the materialized utility of insurance, it is the actual "product" paid for. Claims may be filled by insured directly with the insurer or through brokers or agents. The insurer may require that the claim be filled on its own proprietary forms, or may accept claims on a standard industry form, such as those produced by ACCORD.

Insurance companies claim department employ a large number of claim adjusters supported by a staff of records management and data entry clerks. Incoming claims are classified based on severity and are assigned to adjusters whose settlement authority varies with their knowledge and experience. The adjuster undertake an investigation of each claim, usually in close cooperation with the insured, determines if coverage is available under the terms of the insurance contract, and if so, the reasonable monetary value of the claim, and authorizes payment.

The policy holder may hire their own public adjuster to negotiate with the settlement with the insurance company on their behalf. For policies that are complicated, where claims may be complex, the insured may take out a separate insurance policy add on, called loss recovery insurance, which cover the cost of a public adjuster in the case of a claim.

Adjusting liability insurance claims is particularly difficult because there is a third party involved, the plaintiff, who is under no contractual obligation to cooperate with the insurer and may in fact regard the insurer as a deep pocket. The adjuster must obtain legal counsel for the insured (either inside "house" counsel or outside "panel" counsel), monitor litigation that may take years to complete, and appear in person or over the telephone with settlement authority at a mandatory settlement conference when requested by the judge. If a claims adjuster suspects under-insurance, the condition of average may come into play to limit the insurance company's exposure.

In managing the claims handling function, insurers seek to balance the elements of customer satisfaction, administrative handling expenses, and claims overpayment leakages. As part of this balancing act, fraudulent insurance practices are a major business risk that must be managed and overcome. Dispute between insurers and insured over the validity of claims or claims handling practices occasionally escalate into litigation (see insurance bad faith).

8.11 Marketing

Insurers will often use insurance agents to initially market or underwrite their customers. Agents can be captive, meaning they write only for one company, or independent, meaning that they can issue policies from several companies. the existence and success of companies using insurance agents is likely due to improved and personalized service (Berger, et al 1997).

8.9.4 Types of Business Insurance

Starting a business is all about possibilities, optimism, and promise. But it should also be a time for ensuring protection and security. And that makes a comprehensive package of insurance essential for all small businesses.

The first thing you need to do is to turn off your spigot of unbridled hope for the moment and instead pinpoint just what might go wrong. While that may seem a bit macabre, it is an essential step in identifying those sorts of insurance risk that you will ultimately have to tackle.

Do not limit your risk assessment to what you see yourself. Harper encourages entrepreneurs to have at least two insurance agents conduct their own risk analysis of your business (it is free, so do not be gun-shy about getting two or more analyses). Try to hook with insurance professionals who have worked with your type of business and are experienced in identifying what you need to insure and how much coverage is prudent. Additionally, check with your local town hall or state insurance office, as some communities and states mandate particular forms of insurance coverage.

Although insurance vary widely from one business to the next, here is a quick checklist of policies you will want to consider:

i. **Business Owner Coverage**: Otherwise known as "catch all" coverage, business owner insurance provides damage protection from fire and other mishaps. Owner coverage also offers a degree of liability protection

ii. **Property Insurance**: This can augment the property coverage offered by business owner insurance. Property insurance covers damage to the building that houses your business, as well as to items inside, such as furniture and inventory.

iii. **Liability Insurance**: In our litigation-looped society, this may be as important a form of coverage as you can get. This covers damage to property or injuries suffered by someone else for which you are held responsible. This can take a range of disasters, from the postal worker who sues you for a dog bite incurred during a delivery to your home business, to the clumsy customers who scorches himself after you make your complimentary coffee just too darn hot.

iv. **Product Liability Insurance:** You might want this form of coverage if you make a product that could conceivably harm someone else. For instance, catering businesses worried about some dicey-looking truffles or Brie would do well to tack on this coverage.

v. **Errors and Omissions Insurance**: This coverage is particularly important to service-based businesses, offering protection should you make a mistake or neglect to do something that causes a customer or client some harm. A good example is doctor's medical malpractice insurance, which practice physicians are required to carry.

vi. **Business Income Insurance**: This is disability coverage for your business. This ensures you get paid if you lose income as a result of damage that temporarily shot down or limit you business

vii. **Automobile Insurance**: This item should come as no great surprise. If your business uses cars or trucks in some manner, you have to have this type of insurance for collision and liability coverage.

viii. **Crop insurance**: This may be purchased by farmers to reduce or manage various risks associated with growing crops. Such risks include crop loss or damage caused by weather, hail, drought, frost damage, insect or disease.

ix. **Earthquake insurance**: This is a form of property insurance that pays the policy holder in the event of an earthquake that causes damage to the property. Most ordinary home insurance policies do not cover earthquake damage. Earthquake insurance policies generally feature a high deductible. Rate depends on location and hence the likelihood of an earthquake as well as the construction of the home.

x. **Fidelity bond**: This is a form of casualty insurance that covers policy holders for loss incurred as a result of fraudulent acts by specified individuals. It usually insures a business for losses caused by the dishonest acts of its employees.

xi. **Flood insurance**: This protects against property loss due to flooding. Many insurers in the US do not provide flood insurance in some parts of the country. In response to this, the Federal government created the National Flood Insurance Programme which serves as the insurer of last resort.

xii. **Home insurance**: This is commonly called hazard insurance or home owners insurance (often abbreviated in the real estate industry as HOI), provides coverage for damage or destruction of the policy holder's home. In some geographical areas, the policy may exclude certain types of risks such as flood or earthquake that require additional coverage. Maintenance-related issues are typically the home owner's responsibility. The policy may include inventory, or this can be bought as a separate policy, especially for people who rent housing. In some countries, insurers offer a package which may include liability and legal responsibility for injuries and property damage caused by members of the household, including pets.

xiii. **Landlord insurance**: This covers residential and commercial properties which are rented to others. Most home owner's insurance covers only owner-occupied homes.

xiv. **Marine insurance and marine cargo insurance**: This cover the loss or damage of vessels at sea or on inland waterways and cargo in transit, regardless of the method of transit. When the owner of the cargo and the carrier are separate corporations, marine cargo insurance typically compensates the owner of cargo for losses sustained from fire, ship wreck etc., but excludes losses that can be recovered from the carrier or the carrier's insurance. Many marine insurance underwriters will include "time element" coverage in such policies, which extend the indemnity to cover loss of profit and other business expenses attributable to the delay caused by a covered loss.

xv. **Supplemental natural disaster insurance**: This covers specified expenses after a natural disaster renders the policy holder's home uninhabitable. Periodic payments are made directly to the insured until the home is rebuilt or a specified time period has elapsed.

xvi. **Surety bond insurance**: This is a three-party insurance guaranteeing the performance of the principal.

xvii. **Terrorism insurance**: This provides protection against any loss or damage caused by terrorist activities. In the United States in the wake of 9/11 the Terrorism Risk Insurance Act (2002) set up a federal programme providing a transparent system of shared public and private compensation for insured losses resulting from acts of terrorism. The programme was extended until the end of 2014 by the Terrorist Risk Insurance Programme Reauthorization Act (TRIPRA).

xviii. **Volcano Insurance**: This is a specialised insurance protecting against damage arising specifically from volcanic eruptions.

xix. **Windstorm insurance**: This is an insurance covering the damage that can be caused by wind events such as hurricanes.

Public liability insurance covers a business or organisation against claims should its operation injure a member of the public or damage their property in some way.

xx. **Directors and officers liability insurance (D&O)**: This protects an organization (usually a corporation) from cost associated with litigation resulting from errors made by directors and officers for whom they are liable.

xxi. **Environmental liability insurance**: This protects the insured from bodily injury, property damage and cleanup cost as a result of the dispersal, release or escape pollutants.

xxii. **Errors and omissions insurance (E&O)**: This is a business liability insurance for professionals such as insurance agents, real estate agents and brokers, architects, third party administrators (TPAs) and other business professionals.

xxiii. **Prize indemnity insurance**: This protects the

insured from giving away a large prize at a specific event. Examples would include offering prizes to contestants who can make a half-court shot at a basketball game, or a hole-in-one at a golf tournament.

xxiv. **Professional liability insurance**: This also called professional indemnity insurance (PI), protects insured professional such as architectural corporations and medical practitioners against potential negligence claim made by their patients/clients. Professional liability insurance may take on different names depending on the profession. For example, professional liability insurance in reference to the medical profession may be called medical malpractice insurance. It must be stressed that some of the above discussed insurance policies are not yet introduced in Nigeria; they are in operation in the Western world.

CHAPTER NINE: FEASIBILITY STUDY

9.1 Definition

A feasibility study is an evaluation and analysis of the potential of the proposed project which is based on exclusive investigation and research to give full comfort to the decision makers. Feasibility studies aim to objectively and rationally uncover the strengths and weaknesses of an existing business or proposed venture, opportunities and threats as presented by the environment, the resources required to carry through, and ultimately the prospects for success (Justis and Kreigs Mann, 1979). According to Georgakellos and Mercis (2009), feasibility studies is in simplest terms, the two criteria to judge feasibility are cost required and value to be attained. Young (1970) is of the opinion that a well-designed feasibility study should provide a historical background of the business or project, description of the project or service, accounting statements, details of the operations and management, marketing research and policies, financial data, legal requirements and tax obligations. Generally, feasibility studies precede technical development and project implementation.

9.2 Objective and Unbiased

A feasibility study evaluates the project's potential for success; therefore, the perceived objectivity is an important factor in the credibility to be placed on the study by potential investors and lending institutions. It must therefore, be conducted with an objective, unbiased approach to provide information upon which decisions can be based.

9.3 Five Common Factors

The acronym TELOS refers to the five areas of feasibility, Technical, Economic, Legal, Operational and Scheduling.

9.4 Technical and System Feasibility

The assessment is based on an outline design of system requirements, to determine whether the company has the technical expertise to handle completion of the project. When writing a feasibility report, the following should be taken to consideration.

1. A brief description of the business to access, more possible factors which could affect the study.
2. The part of the business being examined.
3. The human and economic factor.
4. The possible solutions to the problems. At this level, the concern is whether the proposal is both technically and legally feasible (assuming moderate cost).

9.5 Legal Feasibility

Determines whether the proposed system conflicts with legal requirements, e.g. a data processing system must comply with the local Data Processing Acts.

9.6 Operational Feasibility

Operational feasibility is a measure of how well a proposed system solves the problem, and takes advantage of the opportunities identified during scope definition and how it satisfies the requirements in the requirements analysis phase of system development (Michele, 2008)

9.7 Schedule Feasibility

A project can fail if it takes too long to be completed before it is useful. Typically, this means estimating how long the system will take to develop, and it can be completed in a given time period using some methods like payback period. Schedule feasibility is a measure of how reasonable the project timetable is.

Given our technical expertise, are the project deadlines reasonable? Some projects initiated with specific deadlines. You need to determine whether the deadlines are mandatory or desirable.

9.8 Market and Real Estate Feasibility

Market feasibility studies typically involve testing geographical location for a real estate development project and it usually involves parcels of real estate land. Developers often conduct market studies to determine the best location within a jurisdiction, and to test alternative land uses for given parcels. Jurisdictions often required developers to complete feasibility studies before they will approve a permit application for retail, commercial, industrial, manufacturing, housing office or mixed use project market feasibility takes into account the importance of business in the selected area.

9.9 Resources Feasibility

This involves questions such as how much time is available to build the new system, when it can be built, whether it interferes with normal business operations, type and amount of resources required, dependencies etc.

9.10 Cultural feasibility

In this stage, the project alternatives are evaluated for their impact on local and general culture. For example, environmental factors are to be well considered and these factors are to be well known. Furthermore, an enterprise culture can clash with the results of the project.

1. Financial Feasibility in case of a new project, financial viability can be judged on the following parameters:
2. Total estimated cost of the project.
3. Financing of the project in terms of its capital structure, debt equity ratio and promoter's share of total cost

4. Existing investment by promoter in any other business
5. Project cash flow and profitability.

The financial viability of a project should provide the following information;

a. Full details of the asset to be financed and how liquid those assets are.
b. Rate of conversion to cash- liquidity (i.e. how easily can the various assets be converted to cash)
c. Projects funding potential and repayment terms
d. Sensitivity in the repayments capability to the following factor:
- Time delays
- Mild showing of sales
- Acute reduction\ slowing of sales
- Small increase in cost
- Large increase in cost
- Adverse economic conditions

9.11 Market Research Study and Analysis

This is one of the most important sections of the feasibility study as it examines the marketability of the product or services and convinces readers that there is a potential market for the product or services. If a significant market for the product or services cannot be established, then there is no project. Typically, market studies will assess the potential sales of product, absorption and market capture rates and the project's timing.

9.12 Importance of Feasibility Studies

Most organizations, businesses, developers and charities make the mistake of steam rolling into a project without a sound feasibility study. The importance of one cannot be underestimated.

The information you gather and present in your feasibility study will help you:
- List in details all the things you need to make the idea work
- Identify logistical and other problems and solutions
- Develop marketing strategies to convince a donor, bank or investor that your idea that your idea is worth considering as an investment. And
- Serve as a solid foundation for developing your business plan.
- Help to check cost over-run
- Serves as implementation guide to the entrepreneur
- Familiarises the entrepreneur with the environment in which he intends to carry out the business.
- It helps to determine when the business would break

even

- It states the profitability and risk embedded in the business. Also, it helps to determine when the business would break even.

Even if you have a great idea you still have to find a cost-effective way to market and sell your products and services. This is especially important for store-front retail businesses where location could make or break your business.

For example, most commercial space leases space restrictions on businesses that can have a dramatic impact on income. A lease may limit business hours/days, parking spaces, restrict the product or service you can offer and in some cases, even limit the number of customers a business can receive each day.

9.13 Preparation of Feasibility Studies

As much as possible, business and management consultants or other professionals in relevant field should be approached for the preparation of feasibility study. This is especially important as the final report constitutes a vital document that can influence a decision for the possible funding of a project, it therefore needs a professional touch. This not to say that the potential investor is totally free from the burden of assisting in the preparation of the feasibility study. Infact, experience has shown that if the investor is involved, at least in the collection of data, it will help him to understand more what is in the report and then answer questions arising there from. Nonetheless, the consultant will be able to put him through even if he did not participate.

9.14 The Contents of a Feasibility Report

The following items of information are meant as a guide on feasibility report preparation:

1. A brief description of the project
2. A project objective
3. The economic and social justification for the project
4. Organization and management
5. Technical and production consideration
6. Demand and supply outlook
7. Marketing strategy
8. Financial projections and profitability
9. Cost of project
10. Financial plan
11. Risk analysis

The overall company's objectives will be fully integrated into the various aspects listed above. Policies and strategies in terms of human resources, materials and money needed to be formulated where necessary.

9.15 Purpose of the Project

This is to ascertain the viability and profitability of such project as it would enable the company secure financial assistance, partnership, blue-print for efficient implementation of its plan.

9.16 The Objective and Scope

The objective of the study should reflect the purpose for which the owner\investor commissioned the consultant.

9.17 The Business

For an already established business, a brief history of the business will be necessary. The nature of the business, the status of the company, that is, whether it is a limited liability company or not and if it is indigenous or foreign. The total shareholding and its composition, the business head office, directors and their nationality.

For others, personal details of the investor or group of investors will be given. It may be pertinent here to stay that financial institutionus are more favorably disposed towards an incorporated business. Even then some financial institutions have peculiar demands.

9.18 The Project

Here, the project to be undertaken should be clearly described. The product or service should be well defined. The industry to which the business belongs should be well identified. Infact, this is the point where the total project package is considered. For example, if it is a farming project, it should state what type of farming is being contemplated. It could be livestock farming, food crop or integrated farming. The scope of the farm should be stated. However, details of each sub-unit should be discussed under the operational plan.

9.19 Land and Location

The description of the area where the business is or will be located and the plant layout, the size of the land. Right to the land has to be secured either from the state or local government. This is to avoid any possible litigation in considering the land acquisition; the possibility of expansion should be taken into consideration. Agro-projects for example, will acquire land and soil analysis and therefore will need expert advice.

9.20 Operational Plan

The plan of the conversion process and use the goal setting policy making, forecasting, timing and standardization of work should be described. Details of each sub-unit of the project should be discussed. For example, a drug production project may have sub-units for:

a. Tablets production
b. Syrup production
c. Capsule production
d. Sterile products preparation

On the input side of the operation, specific sub-unit requirements should be stated in terms of mutual men and machinery. On the output side, the discussion should include the proposed volume of output and the quality.

The finished goods are storage arrangements should also be considered. This strategic aspect should consider future events and environments, and the layout planning will help to determine the operating cost and their effectiveness.

9.21 Desirability of the Project

Why is the particular project necessary? Of what use is it to the society? Is the product or service actually needed? What is the government policy on similar projects? Is it export-oriented type of enterprise that will earn the country foreign exchange? Is it a product or service that can enhance the quality of life of the citizens and which can guarantee employment?

9.22 Demand and Supply Outlook

There should be a market analysis of the product or service. This is to identify the gap in the supply/demand profile. This sector should also identify the market segment and their composition and competitors of in terms of their names, location, strengths and weaknesses as well as their strategies. Look at the various elements in the environment and then formulate a market strategy to be used. Sales forces have to be done using the marketing strategy of product, pricing distribution and promotion. The forecast demand data will form the basis of revenue projections.

9.23 Management and Manpower Requirement

Much of the successes or failure of the operations will depend upon the ability of the personnel to effect the plan. Personnel planning are therefore vital; this is the reason why it is always considered during the strategic stage in filling in the manpower requirement.

a. Consider the size of the organization
b. The resources of the organization
c. Get high calibre personnel within the limit of

available financial resources.

9.24 Salaries and Benefits

The salaries provisions should take into consideration the manpower projection. Allowance should be made for annual increase in salaries in subsequent years which will be directly related to the qualification of staff, nature of work and occupational hazard therein. For example, annual increase of 10% in total salaries will appear as follows for the next five years if the cost for the first year is 25,000,00

Year	1	2	3	4	5
Cost	N25,000	N27,500	N30,250	N33,275	N36,603

9.25 Administrative Expenses

Administrative expenses can be considered under these heads among others.

(1) Salaries (2) Transportation and vehicle maintenance
(3) Contingencies   (4) Advertising   (5) Utilities
(6) Tax (7) Depreciation expenses

9.26 Production Cost

This includes raw materials input, packaging overhead, repair of production equipment, depreciation etc. these expenses are expected to be projected over a period of time, say five year

9.27 Financial Plan
Initial Investment

A.   Capital project cost

The estimated cost of each of the fixed asset needed

For example

Land and building	230,000
Plant and machinery	160,000
Furniture and equipment	70,000
Motor vehicle	<u>200,000</u>
Total Fixed Capital	<u>860,000</u>

A. A breakdown of the above requirements should be presented as well as the methods of arriving at their estimates.

B. working capital (for the first 6 months)

	N
Material input	50,000
Production overhead	20,000

Administration expenses   <u>60,000</u>
Total Working Capital   <u>130,000</u>

Total initial cost (A+B)   790,000

c. Sources of Fund Schedule

Description	Equity		Liability		
	Existing	New	Loan	Overdraft	Total
Land and Building	-------	120,000	110,000	120,000	230,000
Plant and machinery	20,000	-------	140,000	-------	160,000
Furniture and equipment	30,000	40,000		-------	70,000
Motor vehicle	40,000	-------	160,000	-------	200,000
Working capital	40,000	-------	90,000		130,000
Total	90,000	200,000	410,000	90,000	790,000

Depreciation contribution

		Amount N	percentage %
a.	Capital equity	290,000	37
b.	Loan	410,000	52
c.	Bank overdraft	90,000	11
		790,000	**100**

The above contribution schedule shows

a.   Owner(s) Equity

The owner(s) contribution is of two kinds. One is the value of ₦90,000.00 already in the existing business that where there is an on-going concern, plus, the additional contribution of ₦200,000.00 which they expected to make in term of cash or equipment.

b.   Working capital

1.   Overdraft (short-time loan): the overdraft meant for working capital is expected to be invested in inventory and operating expenses. The ₦90,000.00 overdraft in the above example will be used primarily to meet the initial cash needs.

2.   Loan (long and medium term): in our example, the

enterprise will require a loan of ₦140,000.00 to finance its assets to the following degree

Land and building	110,000
Plant and machinery	140,000
Furniture and equipment	———
Motor vehicle	160,000
	410,000

The company should understand that the financial institution will take care to evaluate or appraise the study time is surely needed in this regard. If the bank requirements are met, less time will be spent before the approval of the loan and such loan application will be granted if the necessary explanation and documents are furnished to the bank at the appropriate time. Apart from the copies of feasibility study, the bank may require tax clearance for the past three years, certificate of incorporation, collateral security and any other information needed by the bank in addition to the loan application form.

9.28 Marketing Strategy

Bit may be necessary to state the main target market at which the enterprise proposes to direct its marketing activities. State if contact is already explored. There is need or statistical data based on field survey to cover consumer, prospective buyers and customers. Products and services rate of consumption, sales potentials and capacity of the plan of the competitors, economic indicators such as rate of unemployment and inflation price index, etc. positioning statement, marketing means, primary, secondary and extension market, target audience is veritable.

Marketing Mix: viz product-branding, packaging, labelling, colour, warranty, size, aroma, taste fragrance.

Pricing – pricing policies and strategy, credit allowances, means of payment etc.

Place - channels **of** distribution, middlemen, transportations, warehouse, storage and communications.

Promotions: advertising, public relations, sales promotions, personal selling and publicity.

9.29 The Projects General Appraisal

The report is usually concluded with the general appraisal of the project, the decision whether or not the project should be undertaken in the light of the merit and characteristics already identified, which may take into account the following factors:

a. The total amount required for initial investment in

both capital and recurrent expenditure profiles.
b. The payback period, that is, the period required to cover the initial investment before thinking of profit generation.
c. The income projections showing the pattern of profit during the period under study.
d. The cash flow projections which the cumulative surplus after year expenses have been met.
e. The employment generation ability of the project.

9.30 Project Evaluation Techniques

In addition to our analysis of the financial requirements, analysis of the profitability of the business is necessary financial analysts have employed some of the following: Net Present Value (NPV) Payback Period (PBP), Internal Rate of Return, Surplus Rate of Return, Accounting Rate of Return, (ARR), Break Even Analysis (BEA) among others (Lawal, 2000).

From the above, it will be easily determined whether or not the project meets the objective for which it is being set up. If it does, it is then recommended as a profit-oriented project for the potential investors or a viable investment for finance.

CHAPTER TEN: TECHNOLOGY

10.1 What is Technology?

Technology can be defined as the application of scientific knowledge gained from scientific research to solve human problem. There are numerous natural and manmade problems facing man in the society, the scientists carry out research from time to time to discover the causes and how these problems could be surmounted. Technology is the facts that emerged from scientific research and it is applied to solve human problem.

Technology can also be defined as a method of doing things. It is the use of scientific knowledge for improving the way to do things - (Answers.com, 2014)

According to Wikipedia, the free encyclopaedia (2014), Technology is the making, modification, usage and knowledge of tools, machines, techniques, crafts, systems and methods of organization, in order to solve a problem, improve pre-existing solution.

10.2 Technology and the Need of Man

Professor Maslow's Hierarchy of needs for Human

Existence puts the sequence as:

a. Basic human needs of food, shelter, warmth and good health;
b. Security needs;
c. Ego needs; and
d. Self actualisation needs.

And so when man talks of adapting situations to his environment, he cannot be talking of adapting "Needs" that he has no use for to suit his environment. Nigerian today (over 90%) still belong to the first and basic need of food, shelter and good health. Therefore my emphasis will be on adaptation of technology to these sectors to the Nigerian environment.

As young graduates wishing to influence the market situation and economy of the the nation, what are your priorities? Questions to ask yourself will now be:

a. What do I intend to produce as a self-employed entrepreneur?
b. Will my product make any impact on my society?
c. What fraction of the population will buy my product?
d. How will this product enhance the image and well-being of the common Nigerian?
e. What is the current technology needed for the

production of this commodity?

f. Are the inputs and outputs adequate for the current level of technology locally?

g. Are there possible alternatives to these inputs and outputs (actually emphasis should be on inputs)?

h. Can I indigenise these inputs to achieve:
    (i) Better self reliance in production,
    (ii) Higher output,
    (iii) Better per unit cost of production,
    (iv) Better profits for myself and the nation,

i. Can this adaptation improve in the near future to compete favourably with technological know-how from the rest of the world?

Whatever is going to be discussed here will fall into the nine major questions asked above. Now, let's take food, health, clothing and shelter points mentioned above.

1. Food

a. What is the current situation in Nigeria today with respect to food production in rural and urban areas?

b. What examples of mal-production practices are abound today?

Brain storm - think of preservation techniques, think of our current technological level in growing, processing and preserving food; think of ways of improving these; think of using local means of preservation.

The Ghanaian Example:

i. 1981 - 1983 (very hard time for the Ghanaians). Sole survival depends on corn (maize) and groundnut soup.

Discussion on how they survived the ordeal

ii. Same period (no adequate funds for drugs from other countries): Use of charcoal from corn cobs, alcohol and a local herb for the cure of acute dysentery, cholera and diarrhoea. The need to develop this to make for permanently effective and accepted cure for diarrhoea and cholera. I am sure this type of innovation has been neglected since 1984 when the economy made a slight U-turn.

The Biafran Examples:

The civil war 1967 - 1970: Brake fluid made from vegetable oil by Biafran soldiers to run cars and vessels. Today we are back to the imported brake fluids. What has happened to the geniuses of the war era?

2. **Health**

Apply the same line of thought to medicine production. Can the FDA and SON be made to be more flexible in their approach to locally manufactured drugs and foods? Can't local herbs (the origin of medicine) be given the priority position they deserve? Can't Nigerians initiative moves to produce drugs in large quantities from herbs, roots, barks and fruits?

3. **Shelter and Clothing**

These two deal mainly with mental acceptance of Nigerians.

Let us now look at the various technological inputs to the production of some of the commodities required to give good shelter, medicine and clothing.

Case Studies

i. You want to produce and sell cloth, buttons, zips, shoes, socks, pants, wrist watches etc, what is involved now and what modifications can be carried out?

ii. You are interested in disinfectants, insecticides, pesticides, herbicides, mosquito coils, soap, oil margarine production etc. What is involved now and what modifications can be carried out?

iii. Fertilizers are needed to replenish food nutrients for plants in the soil. Do we have enough now? Can we afford to import continuously? What are the alternatives? What modifications are needed for the alternatives? The cases for cow dung and water Hyacinth (sea weed)

4. **Security**

Doors, gate, electronic gadgets etc make self appraisal of your intentions and see if any possible modifications are possible. What you want to do is look for simpler modifications for you "developing" conditions

10.3 Aspect of Technology Necessary for Production

1. Building the centre equipment called "Reactor" in chemical processes, "Presses" or "Hammermills" or related equipments in mechanical processes, Main "Transmitter" or major electronic equipment in electrical or electronic processes.

Case Study

a. What do you want to produce? What is the reactor like? Can it be built locally from what? What are the modifications required?
b. What is the reaction or chemistry of production

like? Can this be achieved locally? If not any chemical modification or reformulation that will give the essential ingredients required in the product?

2. Any ancillary or auxiliary inputs, equipments and other inputs to the production? Are there substitutes that can be made locally?

3. What are the energy inputs and the total contribution of energy to total cost of production (Experience has shown that all forms of energy in production, like lighting, heating, electrical appliances etc contribute about 30% - 60% of total cost inputs to production depending on nature of production). Any device to create energy conservation? Any production disciplinary measure to save loss of energy?

4. Total cost of production has been factorised by me into three sub-units:
a. Labour cost contributions
b. Energy cost contributions
c. Capital cost contributions

Energy has been dealt with. What are your plans to obtain effective but cheaper labour inputs to production? Any plan to forestall high labour turn-over in future?

In terms of capital inputs, can the equipments be modified? Can the present highly sophisticated automatic processes be replaced by labour intensive inputs without hindering quality control processes? Can the cost of fabrication of equipments like high pressure vessels, pumps, motors, tanks and the rest, be reduced by using locally available technical know-how?

All the questions above should have about 75% YES - Answer at least for any meaningful entrepreneurship to exist in Nigeria. Any attempt to go into local production with less than 50% of the YES - answers will meet with some forms of handicap in the near future.

REFERENCES

Adeyeye, J. A. And Ditto, J. S. (1982): Essentials of Agricultural Economics Centre for Agric and Rural Development (CARD). University of Ibadan.

Answer.com (2014) What is Technology? Downloaded from wiki.answer.com.

Berger, Allen N., Cummins, J., David; Weiss Mary A. (October, 1997). "The Co-existence of Multiple Distribution Systems for Financial Services: The Case of Property Liability Insurance". Journal of Business 70 (4): 515 - 46.

Collins, O. F. And Moore, D. G. (1964) The Enterprising Man. Michigan State University, East Lansing, MI.

Denbe, A. E.; Boden, L. I. (2000) Moral Hazard: A Question of Morality.

Dictionary.com (2013). Define Corporation. Downloaded from http://www.dictionary.reference.com/browse/corporation.

Georgakellors, D. A. And Mercies, A. M. (2009) Application of the Semantic Learning Approach in the Feasibilities Studies Preparation Training Process. Information System Management 26(3) 231 – 240.

Gollier, C. (2003) To Insure or Not to Insure? An Insurance Puzzle. The Geneva papers on Risk and Insurance Theory

Irish Brokers Association. https://iba.le

Justis, R. T. and Kreigsmann, B. (1979) The Feasibility Study as a Tool for Venture Analysis. Business Journal of Small Business Management 26(3) 231 – 240.

Kanreuther, H. (1996) Mitigating Disaster Losses Through Insurance. Journal of Risk and Uncertainty, 12: 171 - 187.

Lawal, T. (2000) A – Z Concept of Finance. Lizzy Jazz: Ibadan.

Michelle, B. (2008) Initiating Phase-Feasibility Studies Request and Report. Downloaded from http://www.pmhut.com.

Obasan, A. O. (2001) Small Business Management: An Entrepreneurial Approach. Lagos: High Education Books Publisher.

Obikoya, S. (1995) in Asoga-Allen, K. (2011) Introduction to Entrepreneurial Skills 1. A handout prepared for Ekiti State University students, Michael Otedola College of Primary Education Campus, Noforija-Epe.

Oludele, P. (1988) in Obasan, A. O. (2001) Small Business Management: An Entrepreneurial Approach. Lagos: High Education Books Publisher.

Oyedijo, F. (1991) in Asoga-Allen, K. (2012) Introduction to Entrepreneurial Skills II. A handout prepared for

Ekiti State University students, Michael Otedola College of Primary Education Campus, Noforija-Epe.

Wikipedia, the Free Encyclopedia (2013) Corporation. Downloaded from http://en.wikipedia.org/wiki/corporation.

Wikipedia, the Free Encyclopedia (2013) What is Technology? Downloaded from http://en.wikipedia.org/wiki/technology.

Wikipedia.com (2013) Theory. Downloaded from http://en.wikipedia.org/wiki/theory.

Young, G. I. M. (1970) Feasibility Studies Appraisal Journal 38 (3) 376 – 383.

Index

A

Abuja, 34
Accountants, 60
Achievement, 18, 27
Adhoc Act, 43
Advantages, 38, 39, 43
Advertisement, 52
Agricultural, 125
America, 28
Analysis, 21, 67, 102, 126
Announcement, 53
Answer.com (2014), 125
Application, 126
Association, 79, 86, 126
Authors, 19

B

Behavioural, 18, 21
Being, 17
Benefits, 110
Better, 33
Business, 17, 31, 32, 52, 53, 59, 71, 72, 73, 74, 84, 89, 90, 91, 106, 125, 126

C

Calculable loss, 77
Capital, 23, 78
Central Bank, 36
Characteristics, 18
Competition, 51
Cooperative, 44, 45, 46

Corporation, 42, 43, 125, 127

Cultural, 101

Cumbersome, 30

D

Decision, 27

Decision making, 27

Demand, 109

Democracy, 46

Demographics, 33

Determinants, 20

Determination, 22

Development, 29, 125

Disadvantages, 17, 38, 40, 43

Disagreement, 40

Dissatisfaction, 22

Dividends, 46

E

Earthquake, 92

Economic, 25

Economic incentives, 25

Entrepreneur, 15, 22, 29

Entrepreneurship, 14, 18, 20, 25, 26

Experiment, 29

F

Factors, 48, 50, 99

Feasibility Study, 126

Food items, 35

G

General, 40, 41, 115
General partners, 40, 41
Government, 20, 33, 36, 78
Graduation, 19

H

High interest rate, 30
Higher, 16
Human, 3

I

Idea generation, 69
Ideas, 69
Ijebu, 32
Imaginative, 18
Implementation, 22
Information, 126
Infrastructural, 30
Innovative, 19, 69
Instability, 17
Insurable, 78, 79
Insurance, 70, 71, 72, 73, 74, 76, 82, 83, 85, 89, 90, 91, 92, 94, 95, 125, 126
Insurer, 84, 86
Irish Brokers, 79, 126

J

Japan, 20

L

Labour, 50
Lagos, 34, 126, 127
Land, 107
Leadership, 18
Liability, 90, 91, 125
Limited, 38, 40, 41, 46, 78
Limited capital, 38
Limited partners, 40, 41
London, 75, 86

M

Maintenance, 93
Management, 18, 21, 23, 45, 109, 126, 127
Market, 64, 69, 100, 102
Market research, 64
McClelland, 28
Motivation, 25, 27, 28

N

Nigerian, 4, 5
Nigerianization, 58
Nominal partners, 40, 41
Numerous, 69

O

Obasan (2001), 40
Obikoya, 57, 126
Opportunities, 31, 32
Organizing ability, 18
Oyedijo, 58, 127

P

Principles, 74
Process, 126
Products, 67, 68
Promotion, 48
Property, 90, 125
Proprietorship, 37, 38
Psychological, 26
Psychological theory, 26

Q

Question, 125

R

Radio, 54
Rakinada Experiment, 28
Requirements, 31
Researchers, 20
Resources, 101
Risk, 16, 17, 70, 75, 94, 126
Risk management, 70
Risk of failure, 17
Roman law, 42

S

Seasonality, 36
Secret partners, 40, 41
Societal values, 26
Society, 20, 44
Sociological, 25
Sociological theory, 25

Sole proprietorship, 38
Staffing, 48, 49, 50, 51
Subrogation, 80
Successful, 16
Succession, 59
Supply, 109

T

Technical, 18, 99
Technological changes, 33
Technology, 49, 117, 118, 122, 125, 127
Theory, 25, 26, 27, 28, 126, 127
Traditional beliefs, 29
Trainees, 28

U

Umbrella, 36
Uncertainty, 126
Unemployment, 4
US, 78, 92
Utmost good faith, 79

V

Value, 18
Venture, 126
Viable, 31

W

Wages, 50
working capital, 35
Worldwide, 17

www.ingramcontent.com/pod-product-compliance
Lightning Source LLC
Chambersburg PA
CBHW070254190526
45169CB00001B/413

1

Healthcare Sector in India

The State legislature is empowered to make laws related to Public health and sanitation; hospitals and dispensaries[1] and the Central Government on certain related subjects.[2] The Right to health is a constitutional right under Article 39(e)(f),[3] Article 42,[4] Article 47.[5] The World Health Organization's definition of health is commonly accepted definition of health, it says,

"Health is a state of complete physical, mental and social well-being and not merely the absence of disease or infirmity."[6]

---

[1] List II.- State List, entry 6
[2] List III.- Concurrent List, entry no 23, 26 and 29
[3] (e) that the health and strength of workers, men and women, and the tender age of children are not abused and that citizens are not forced by economic necessity to enter avocations unsuited to their age or strength;
(f) that children are given opportunities and facilities to develop in a healthy manner and in conditions of freedom and dignity and that childhood and youth are protected against exploitation and against moral and material abandonment.
[4] Provision for just and humane conditions of work and maternity relief.—The State shall make provision for securing just and humane conditions of work and for maternity relief.
[5] Duty of the State to raise the level of nutrition and the standard of living and to improve public health.—The State shall regard the raising of the level of nutrition and the standard of living of its people and the improvement of public health as among its primary duties and, in particular, the State shall endeavour to bring about prohibition of the consumption except for medicinal purposes of intoxicating drinks and of drugs which are injurious to health
[6] Preamble to the Constitution of the World Health Organization as adopted by the International Health Conference, New York, 19-22 June, 1946; signed on 22 July 1946 and entered into force on 7 April 1948

The Supreme Court of India in *Paschim Banga Khet Mazdoorsamity vs. State of West Bengal,*[7] has explained the role of the State in relation to health care facility,

> *"The Constitution envisages the establishment of a welfare state at the federal level as well as at the state level. In a welfare state the primary duty of the Government is to secure the welfare of the people. Providing adequate medical facilities for the people is an essential part of the obligations undertaken by the Government in a welfare state. The Government discharges this obligation by running hospitals and health centres which provide medical care to the person seeking to avail those facilities.*
>
> *Article 21 imposes an obligation on the State to safeguard the right to life of every person. Preservation of human life is thus of paramount importance. The Government hospitals run by the State and the medical officers employed therein are duty bound to extend medical assistance for preserving human life. Failure on the part of a Government hospital to provide timely medical treatment to a person in need of such treatment results in violation of his right to life guaranteed under Article 21..."*

The right to health is now universally recognized and provision of adequate a health care is one of the essential preconditions for sustained and equitable economic growth.

---

[7] 1996 SCC (4)37

The core content of health care and progressive realization of the right to health The State is duty-bound legally to provide for basic minimum rights for securing health, including easily accessible and affordable, good quality health care for all.[8]

The Central Government's Draft National Health Policy[9] has proposed a target of increasing public health expenditure from current 1.25% to 2.5% of GDP. Further, the Government is proposing the National Health Rights Act, which will make health as a fundamental right and thus denial of it will be justifiable.[10]

Health Care Sector

The India's health care industry has become one of the largest sectors in terms of revenue and employment. According to a report, the Indian healthcare market is worth 100$ billion and is expected to grow at US $ 280 billion by 2020.[11] India's health care sector comprises of public and private hospitals.

The public health care system focuses mainly on providing basic health care facility through the Primary Health Centre and secondary and tertiary care system in key cities.[12]

---

[8] *Pawar Sujata*, State responsibility for ensuring health care, (2011) PL Janurary
[9] http://www.mohfw.nic.in/showfile.php?lid=3014
[10] http://timesofindia.indiatimes.com/india/Draft-National-Health-Policy-proposes-making-health-a-fundamental-right/articleshow/45712774.cms
[11] http://www.ibef.org/industry/healthcare-india.aspx
[12] http://www.cci.in/pdfs/surveys-reports/Healthcare-Telemedicine-and-Medical-Tourism-in-India.pdf

Thus the private sector plays an important role in the Indian health care sector, which mainly comprises of nursing homes and mid tier and top tier private hospitals. In India, Private sector health care account for almost 74% of the country health care expenditure and private sector in hospital is 70% and hospital bed is 40%.[13]

The medical tourism[14] or health tourism refers to travelling into another country for medical treatment. According to a newspaper report every year about 7 million people travel for medical care across the globe and 400,000 people travelled to India[15] making India one of the top destinations for medical tourism and is India's medical tourism is expected to reach $6 billion by 2018.[16]

The Government of India in order to promote India as a credible medical tourism destination has constituted 'Medical and Wellness Tourism Board'.[17] The Board has emphasized that India has a huge potential for medical tourism essentially due to the availability of well trained medial professional and cost competitiveness in comparison to other countries.[18]

---

[13] http://www.ibef.org/download/Healthcare-August-2015.pdf
[14] Tourist travel for the purpose of receiving medical treatment or improving health or fitness, http://dictionary.reference.com/browse/health--tourism
[15] International medical tourism industry pegged at USD 40 billion a year', Economic Times, 27 June 2013
[16] http://www.livemint.com/Home-Page/NX5IF0yZtnkCFz4vzxtt5N/India-medical-tourism-industry-to-reach-6-billion-by-2018.html
[17] The Board has representatives from Government departments, tourism and hospitality sectors, Indian Medical Association (IMA) and experts in various disciplines including wellness and Yoga and other stakeholders. http://www.financialexpress.com/article/travel/latest-updates-travel/national-medical-wellness-tourism-promotion-board-holds-its-first-meeting/194744/
[18] http://pib.nic.in/newsite/PrintRelease.aspx?relid=134430

2

Meaning of Biomedical Waste

India's economic growth has increased the demand for better health care and medical facility. The growth of hospitals and private clinics are definitely a sign of better health care facilities, however, this has also increased the concern of generation of biomedical waste and its safe disposal.

The Government in order to resolve this issue, had notified the Biomedical Waste (Management and handing) Rules, 1998 under the Environment (Protection) Act, 1986.[1]

India

The Biomedical Waste (Management and handing) Rules, 1998 defines biomedical waste as,

'Any waste, which is generated during the diagnosis, treatment or immunization of human beings or animals or in research activities pertaining thereto or in the production or testing of Biologicals, and including categories mentioned in Schedule I'[19]

---

[19] Rule 3(5) of the Biomedical Waste (Management and handing) Rules, 1998

A biomedical is also known as an infectious waste, medical waste,[20] health care waste[21] and clinical waste.

United Kingdom

The Controlled Waste Regulations 1992[22] of UK, defines clinical waste as,

a) Any waste which consists wholly or partly of human or animal tissue, blood or other body fluids, excretions, drugs or other pharmaceutical products, swabs or dressings, or syringes, needles or other sharp instruments, being waste which unless rendered safe may prove hazardous to any person coming into contact with it; and

(b) Any other waste arising from medical, nursing, dental, veterinary, pharmaceutical or similar practice, investigation, treatment, care, teaching or research, or the collection of blood for transfusion, being waste which may cause infection to any person coming into contact with it;

---

[20] http://www.ehow.com/about_5452204_biomedical-waste-definition.html
[21] Healthcare waste (HCW) is defined as the total waste stream from a healthcare facility (HCF) http://www.healthcare-waste.org/basics/definitions/
[22] http://www.legislation.gov.uk/uksi/1992/588/regulation/1/made

United States

The Medical Waste Tracking Act of 1988 defines medical waste as "any solid waste that is generated in the diagnosis, treatment, or immunization of human beings or animals, in research pertaining thereto, or in the production or testing of biological."

This definition includes, but is not limited to:
Blood-soaked bandages
Culture dishes and other glassware
Discarded surgical gloves
Discarded surgical instruments
Discarded needles used to give shots or draw blood (e.g., medical sharps)
Cultures, stocks, swabs used to inoculate cultures
Removed body organs (e.g., tonsils, appendices, limbs)
Discarded lancets[23]

Thus the term 'Biomedical Waste' is referred by different names worldwide and in broadly it is waste generated during the process of medical actions such diagnosis, treatment of humans or animal and includes testing and research activities.

---

[23] http://www3.epa.gov/epawaste/nonhaz/industrial/medical/

The Biomedical Waste (Management and Handling) Rules, 1998

The Biomedical Waste (Management and Handling) Rules, 1998 was notified in the Gazette on 16 October, 1997 by the Central Government under Section 6[24], 8[25] and 25[26] of the Environment (Protection) Act, 1986.

Applicability

The Biomedical Waste (Management and Handling) Rules, 1998 is applicable to all persons who generate, collect, receive, store, transport, treat, dispose and handle biomedical waste.

Definitions

The Biomedical Waste (Management and Handling) Rules, 1998 defines important terms like authorized person,[27] biomedical waste,[28] biological,[29] biomedical waste treatment facility,[30] occupier.[31]

---

[24] Rules to regulate environmental pollution
[25] Persons handling hazardous substances to comply with procedural safeguards
[26] Power to make rules
[27] Rule 3(3) of The BioMedical Waste (Management and Handling) Rules, 1998
[28] Rule 3(5) of The BioMedical Waste (Management and Handling) Rules, 1998
[29] Rule 3(6) of The BioMedical Waste (Management and Handling) Rules, 1998
[30] Rule 3(7) of The BioMedical Waste (Management and Handling) Rules, 1998
[31] Rule 3(8) of The BioMedical Waste (Management and Handling) Rules, 1998

Provision

The Biomedical Waste (Management and Handling) Rules, 1998 casts a duty upon the occupier of an institution generating biomedical waste to ensure that such waste is handled without any adverse effect to human health and the environment. The term 'occupier' includes hospitals, nursing homes, clinic, dispensary, veterinary institution, animal house etc.

The increasing health care facility is a sign of growth of medical development in the country, however, it also raises concerns of safe disposal of biomedical waste.

The rules 5 of the Biomedical Waste (Management and Handling) Rules, 1998 provides that the biomedical waste shall be treated and disposed in accordance with Schedule 1 and according to standard prescribed in Schedule V.

The Rule 5 (2) prescribes a time Schedule[32] to set up biomedical waste treatment facility or to ensure that the biomedical waste is sent for disposal at a common waste treatment facility.

The segregation, packaging, transportation and storage are important steps for safe and proper disposal.

---

[32] Provided under Schedule VI

The rule 6 (1) provides that it shall not be mixed with other wastes and shall be segregated into containers or bags at the point of generation[33] and according to schedule II.

The container used for transportation of biomedical waste shall be labelled in accordance with Schedule III and shall also carry information as per Schedule IV.

The transportation of biomedical waste to the waste treatment facility shall be done only through vehicle authorized for this purpose by the competent authority[34] and untreated waste shall not be kept beyond a period of 48 hours.[35]

The Government establishes a prescribed authority for granting authorization and implementation of the Biomedical Waste (Management and Handling) Rules, 1998.[36]

The prescribed authority has power to cancel or suspend the authorization if the occupier fails to comply with the provisions of the rules.[37]

---

[33] Rule 6 (2) of the Biomedical Waste (Management and Handling) Rules, 1998
[34] Rule 4 of the Biomedical Waste (Management and Handling) Rules, 1998
[35] Rule 5 of the Biomedical Waste (Management and Handling) Rules, 1998
[36] Rule 7 (1) of the Biomedical Waste (Management and Handling) Rules, 1998
[37] Rule 8 of the Biomedical Waste (Management and Handling) Rules, 1998

The occupier of the institution,[38] including operator operator of a biomedical waste facility[39] generating, collecting, receiving, storing, transporting, treating, disposing or handling biomedical waste and treating less than 1000 patients per month shall apply for authorization the prescribed authority.

The Government shall constitute an advisory committee consisting of experts in the field of medical and health, environmental management, etc., to advise the Government on the implementation of these rules.[40]

The occupier or operator of biomedical waste treatment plant shall submit[41] an annual report and shall contain information on about categories and quantities of biomedical waste.[42]

The authorized person shall maintain a record of the generation, collection, reception, storage, transportation, treatment and disposal of biomedical waste which shall be inspected by the prescribed authority.[43]

---

[38] Application in Form 1
[39] Rule 8 (2) of the Biomedical Waste (Management and Handling) Rules, 1998
[40] Rule 9 of the Biomedical Waste (Management and Handling) Rules, 1998
[41] By Janurary of every year
[42] Rule 10 of the Biomedical Waste (Management and Handling) Rules, 1998
[43] Rule 11 of the Biomedical Waste (Management and Handling) Rules, 1998

The authorized person shall report any accident at the facility or institution during handling or transportation to the prescribed authority.[44]

An appeal can be preferred within 30 days from an order made by the prescribed authority under these rules to the authority constituted for this purpose.[45]

---

[44] Rule 12 of the Biomedical Waste (Management and Handling) Rules, 1998
[45] Rule 13 of the Biomedical Waste (Management and Handling) Rules, 1998

Courtesy - The Madhya Pradesh Pollution Control Board[46]

SALIENT FEATURES OF BIO-MEDICAL WASTE (MANAGEMENT AND HANDLING) RULES 1998

a) It is Published by Govt. of India, under Section 6 & 25 of Environmental Protection Act 1986 on 20/7/98 and appeared in official gazette of India on 27/7/98.

b) It deals with the generation/handling/treatment/disposal of Bio Medical Waste.

c) These rules apply to all persons who generate, collect, receive, store, transport, treat, dispose or handle bio-medical waste in any form.

d) Rule 4 specify duty of occupier (generator) to take all steps to ensure that such waste is handled without any adverse effect to human health and the environment.

e) Rule 5 and 6 specifies waste management procedures.

f) Section 7 is about prescribed authority that shall implement these rules. The Pollution Control Board of the State has been declared as prescribed authority by the State Government.

g) These rules apply to all persons who generate, collect, receive, store, transport, treat, dispose or handle bio-medical Waste in any form. Every occupier of an institution generating, collecting, receiving, storing, transporting, treating disposal and for handling Bio-medical waste in any other manner, except such occupier of clinics, dispensaries, pathological laboratories, blood banks providing treatment/service to less than 1000 patients per month.The operators of Biomedical waste facility are also covered under these rules.

h) Form 1 is fixed for application of authorization. Government is to prescribe necessary fee.

i) An advisory Committee as required under rule 9 is to be constituted.

j) As per these rules, it shall be the duty of every occupier {as defined in rule 3(8)} of an institution generating bio-medical waste which includes a hospital, nursing home, clinic dispensary, veterinary institution, animal house, pathological laboratory blood bank by what ever name called to take all steps to ensure that such waste is handled without any adverse effect to human health and the environment

---

[46] http://www.mppcb.nic.in/bio-medical_waste.htm

4

Treatment and Disposal of Biomedical Waste

The Biomedical Waste (Management and Handling) Rules, 1998 provides that biomedical waste shall be treated and disposed in accordance in accordance with Schedule I of the Act and in compliance with the standards prescribed in Schedule V.[47]

Every occupier is required to set up a required biomedical waste treatment facilities like incinerator, autoclave, microwave system for the treatment of biomedical waste or ensure treatment of biomedical waste at a common biomedical waste treatment facility.

The occupier has to either install treatment facilities or send biomedical waste to common waste treatment facility.[48] In Satara city, a biomedical

---

[47] Bio-medical waste shall be treated and disposed of in accordance with Schedule I, and in compliance with the standards prescribed in Schedule V.

[48] Every occupier, where required, shall set up in accordance with the time-schedule in Schedule VI, requisite bio-medical waste treatment facilities like incinerator, autoclave, microwave system for the treatment of waste, or, ensure requisite treatment of waste at a common waste treatment facility or any other waste treatment facility.

waste is disposed at common biomedical waste treatment facility operated by Nature in Need at Songoan, Jakatwadi, Satara.[49]

The Central Pollution Control Board[50] (CPCB) has prescribed guidelines for the installation of Common Biomedical Waste Treatment Facilities including design and construction of Incinerators.[51]

Health being a State subject[52] matter, the State Government has to take necessary steps for monitoring the disposal of biomedical wastes through the State Pollution Control Boards (SPCBs) and Pollution Control Committees (PCCs).

The State Pollution Control Boards (SPCBs) and Pollution Control Committees (PCCs) are the prescribed authorities to grant authorization and empowered to ensure the compliance of the provisions of these Rules.[53]

As per the National Guidelines for the Hospital Waste Management, the Head of the hospital shall form a waste Management Committee under his Chairmanship and shall meet regularly to review the performance of the waste disposal. The Committee is also responsible

---

[49] http://ahosatara.org/index.php/menu-types-2/nature-in-need
[50] http://cpcb.nic.in/
[51] http://www.cpcb.nic.in/wast/bioimedicalwast/Rev_Draft_Gdlines_CBWTFs_26022014.pdf
[52] Seventh Schedule, Constitution of India, List II, Public health and sanitation; hospitals and dispensaries.
[53] The Government of every State and Union Territory shall establish a prescribed authority with such members as may be specified for granting authorisation and implementing these rules. If the prescribed authority comprises of more than one member, a chairperson for the authority shall be designated.

for making action plans for hospital waste management and for its supervision, monitoring implementation and looking after the safety of the bio-medical waste handlers.[54]

A biomedical waste consists of different types of wastes like human anatomy, animal wastes, waste sharps, discarded medicines, etc. The treatment and disposal of biomedical waste are an important process and in order to abridge this process the biomedical waste is categorized into different categories[55] based on the types of waste.

The Biomedical Waste (Management and Handling) Rules, 1998 in its Schedule I have provided ten categories along with treatment and disposal options.

---

[54] http://pib.nic.in/newsite/PrintRelease.aspx?relid=86907

Categories of biomedical waste schedule – I[56]

CATEGORIES OF BIO MEDICAL WASTE

OPTION	WASTE CATEGORY	TREATMENT & DISPOSAL
Category No. 1	Human Anatomical Waste	Incineration / deep burial
Category No. 2	Animal Waste	Incineration / deep burial
Category No. 3	Microbiology & Biotechnology Waste	Local autoclaving / microwaving / incineration
Category No. 4	Waste Sharps	Disinfection by chemical treatmet / atoclaving / microwaving and mutilation / shredding
Category No. 5	Discarded Medicines and Cytoxic drugs	Incineration / destruction and drugs disposal in secured landfills
Category No. 6	Solid Waste	Incineration / autoclaving / microwaving
Category No. 7	Solid Waste	Disinfection by chemical treatment / autoclaving / microwaving and mutilation / shredding
Category No. 8	Liquid Waste	Disinfection by chemical treatment and discharge into drains.
Category No. 9	Incineration Ash	Disposal in municipal landfill
Category No. 10	Chemical Waste	Chemical treatment and discharge into drains for liquids and secured land for solids

---

[55] Into ten category
[56] http://www.slideshare.net/swapna123/2-55199105

5

Segregation, Packaging, Transportation and Storage

The biomedical waste is segregated into container/ bags according to rules provided under rule 6 of the bio-medical rules.[57] It provides that, following rules have to be followed at the point of generation and in its storage, transportation, treatment and disposal.

(1) The biomedical waste shall not be mixed with other wastes. It shall not be mixed with municipal waste and shall be kept from other types of waste.[58]

(2) Biomedical waste shall be segregated into containers/bags at the point of generation in accordance with Schedule II, prior to its storage, transportation, treatment and disposal. The containers shall be labeled according to Schedule III.[59] The segregation of bio-medical waste is an important element in the collection of biomedical waste.

---

[57] Segregation, packaging, transportation and storage
[58] Rule 6(1) of the Biomedical Waste (Management and Handling) Rules, 1998
[59] Rule 6(2) of the Biomedical Waste (Management and Handling) Rules, 1998

(3) If a container is transported from the premises where bio-medical waste is generated to any waste treatment facility outside the premises, it shall contain information as per Schedule IV, along with the label prescribed in Schedule III.[60]

(4) The untreated biomedical waste shall be transported only in such vehicle as may be authorized for the purpose by the competent authority as specified by the government.[61]

(5) No untreated bio-medical waste shall be kept or stored beyond a period of 48 hours.[62]

The rules provide that if for any reason it becomes necessary to store the waste beyond such period, the authorized person must take permission of the prescribed authority and take measures to ensure that the waste does not adversely affect human health and the environment.[63]

The rule 6 prescribes labeling of container according schedule III. The bio-medical waste is to be labeled according to Schedule III and if a container is transported from the premises where bio-medical waste is generated to any waste treatment facility outside the premises, the container shall also carry information prescribed in Schedule IV.

---

[60] Rule 6(3) of the Biomedical Waste (Management and Handling) Rules, 1998
[61] Rule 6(4) of the Biomedical Waste (Management and Handling) Rules, 1998
[62] Rule 6(5) of the Biomedical Waste (Management and Handling) Rules, 1998

The container labeled shall be wash proof and prominently visible. It shall have the date, name, address, phone of the sender and receiver.

Schedule II[64]

Schedule II: Colour Coding and Type Of Container for Disposal of Bio-Medical Wastes

Colour Coading	Type of Containers	Waste Category	Treatment Options as per Schedule 1
Yellow	Plastic bag Disinfected	1,2,3,6	Incineration/deep burial
Red	Disinfected Container/Plastic bag	3,6,7	Autoclaving/Micro waving/Chemical Treatment
Blue/White Translucent	Plastic bag/puncture proof container	4,7	Autoclaving/Micro waving/chemical treatment and destruction/shredding
Black	Plastic bag	5,9,10 (solid)	Disposal in second landfill

Schedule III[65]

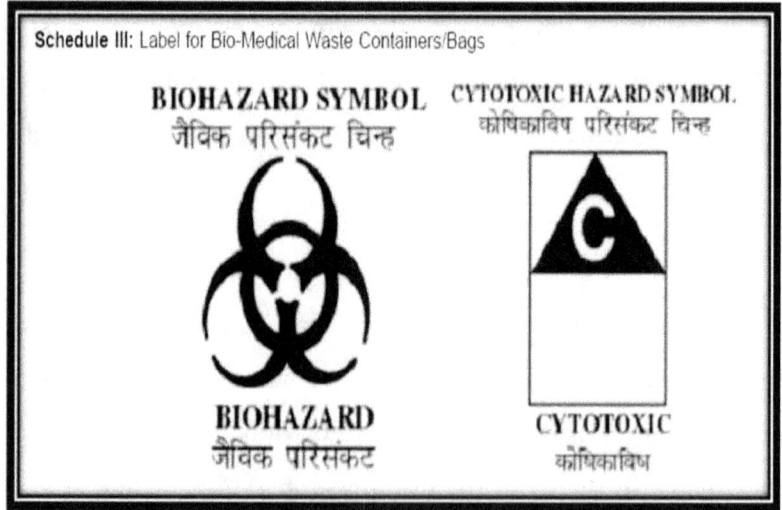

Schedule III: Label for Bio-Medical Waste Containers/Bags

---

[63] ibid
[64] http://www.cwejournal.org/vol7no1/need-of-biomedical-waste-management-system-in-hospitals-an-emerging-issue-a-review/
[65] http://www.cwejournal.org/vol7no1/need-of-biomedical-waste-management-system-in-hospitals-an-emerging-issue-a-review/

Schedule - IV[66]

SCHEDULE-IV
LABEL FOR TRANSPORT OF BIO-MEDICAL WASTE CONTAINERS/BAGS

Label shall be non-washable & prominently visible

Day................... Month...............
Year..................
Date of generation.......................

Waste Category No...................
Waste quantity.........................
Sender's Name and Address   Receiver's Name and Address
Phone No.........   Phone No..................
Telex No...........   Telex No....................
Fax No..............   Fax No........................
Contact Person..........   Contact Person........
In case of emergency please contact
Name and Address:
Phone No.

---

[66] http://www.slideshare.net/dranwarahmad/bio-medical-waste

6

Common Biomedical Waste Treatment Facility

The rule 5 of the Biomedical Waste (Management and Handling) Rules, 1998 provides treatment and disposal of biomedical waste in accordance with schedule I and with the compliance of standards given in schedule V.

It provides that every occupier shall set up in accordance with the time-schedule given under Schedule VI, biomedical waste treatment facilities like incinerators, autoclave, microwave system for the treatment of waste, or, ensure requisite treatment of waste at a Common Biomedical Waste Treatment Facility (CBWTF).[67]

The Biomedical Waste (Management and Handling) Rules, 1998 state that every Health care establishment has to set up requisite biomedical waste treatment facilities like incinerators, autoclave, microwave system for the treatment of waste, or should ensure requisite treatment of waste at a common waste treatment facility or any other waste treatment facility.

---

[67] Rule 5 of the Biomedical Waste (Management and Handling) Rules, 1998

Installation of individual treatment facilities by every health care unit requires comparatively high capital investment and thus is not a viable option.

In addition, it requires separate human power and infrastructure for proper operation and maintenance of treatment systems.
The concept of Common Biomedical Waste Treatment Facility (CBWTF) not only addresses such problems but also prevents proliferation of treatment facilities in a city, which themselves can be a source of hazard and infection if not maintained well.[68]

To help in setting up new CBWTFs, monitoring and evaluation of existing ones, Central Pollution Control Board (CPCB) has brought out Guidelines for BMW Treatment Facilities. The following are important guidelines for common biomedical treatment facilities issued by the Central Pollution Control Board.[69]

Location of CBWTF
The CBWTF shall be located near the area of operation to avoid travel distance in waste collection and thereby enhancing operational flexibility, however, it shall be located at a place reasonably far away from residential and sensitive area so that it has minimal impact on these areas. It can also be established in industrial areas.

---

[68] http://www.bmwmindia.org/index_CBWTF.html
[69] Based on Guidelines for Common Bio-medical Waste Treatment Facilities, February 26, 2014

Land requirement

The land should be adequately allocated for CBWTF to provide all requisite systems to include space for storage, waste treatment facilities, ETP, vehicle washing and parking space. A minimum of 1 acre land area shall be used to set up CBWTF be set up.

Coverage area of CBWTF

The guidelines suggest coverage area of a CBWTF as follows:

(i) Only one CBWTF shall be allowed to cater up to 10,000 beds at the approved rate by the Prescribed Authority.

(ii) A CBWTF not allowed to cater health care units situated beyond a radius of 150 km. However, in an area where 10,000 beds are not available within prescribed limits a CBWTF shall be allowed to cater the health care units situated outside the said 150 KM.

(iii) In case of number of beds exceeds more than 10,000 beds, one more CBWTF shall be allowed to cater additional need.

(iv) These rules has been relaxed for North Eastern States/ Hilly states where district wise CBWTF is allowed to be established.

Treatment equipment

The Common Biomedical Waste Treatment Facility (CBWTF) shall have treatment facilities like incineration, Plasma Pyrolysis, Autoclaving/ Microwaving / Hydroclaving, Chemical disinfection, Shredder, Sharp pit/ Encapsulation, Deep burial.

Out these deep burial is allowed only in CBWTF located in hilly areas.

Infrastructure

The infrastructure of CBWTF shall consist of treatment equipment room, main waste storage room, treated waste storage room, administrative room etc.

Collection of biomedical waste

As per the Biomedical Waste (Management and Handling) Rules, 1998, the generator of the waste shall segregate the biomedical waste in accordance with the provisions of the said rules.

Further the CBWTF operator can refuse to accept non segregated waste and shall report shall matter to the prescribed authority.

The vehicles used for the transportation of the biomedical waste should be owned by the CBWTF operator. Such vehicles shall be fully covered.

Cost

The cost is charged from the health care units and is fixed based on the recommendation of the State Pollution Control Board (SPCB)/Pollution Control Committee (PCC) and the local Medical Association. The following criteria are applied while fixation of the cost,

Fixed charges in the case of the nursing homes/clinics/Sample Collection Centers/Dental Centers;

Fixed charges per bed basis to the low bed strength hospitals (up to 30 beds)

Charges based on the weight basis;

Charges to the hospitals having 30 or more beds.
The charges are revised once in two years.

7

International Convention on Environment Protection

United Nations Conference on the Human Environment

The first United Nations Conference on the Human Environment[70] (UNCHE) was held in Stockholm, Sweden from June 5 to June 16, 1972. It was the one the key conference of United Nation, which turned out as a milestone on the environmental issues.

Following this conference, the United Nations Environmental Programme[71] (UNEP). It proclaimed that

"Man is both creature and molder of his environment, which gives him physical sustenance and affords him the opportunity for intellectual, moral, social and spiritual growth.

---

[70] Stockholm from 5 to 16 June 1972
[71] UNEP, established in 1972, is the voice for the environment within the United Nations system

In the long and tortuous evolution of the human race on this planet a stage has been reached when, through the rapid acceleration of science and technology, man has acquired the power to transform his environment in countless ways and on an unprecedented scale. Both aspects of man's environment, the natural and the man-made, are essential to his well-being and to the enjoyment of basic human rights the right to life its[72]

The conference formed the "Framework for Environmental Action," an action plan containing 109 specific recommendations related to human settlements, natural-resource management, and pollution, educational and social aspects of the environment, development, and international organizations.[73]

United Nations Conference on Environment and Development

United Nations Conference on Environment and Development, also known as the The Earth Summit was held in Rio de Janeiro from 3-14 June, 1992.[74]

This conference is also at Rio conference. The main theme of the conference was 'Environment and sustainable development' was attended by Some 2,400 representatives of non-governmental organizations 17,000 people attended the parallel NGO Forum.[75]

---

[72] http://www.unep.org/Documents.Multilingual/Default.asp?documentid=97&articleid=1503
[73] https://www.britannica.com/topic/United-Nations-Conference-on-the-Human-Environment
[74] http://www.un.org/geninfo/bp/enviro.html
[75] *ibid*

The conference led to the establishment of the Commission on Sustainable Development. This was an important event leading to the adoption of three major agreements,

1) Rio Declaration, a series of principles.

2) Agenda 21, a global action plan.

3) Forest Principles, principles on forest management worldwide.[76]

Principle 15 states

In order to protect the environment, the precautionary approach shall be widely applied by States according to their capabilities. Where there are threats of serious or irreversible damage, lack of full scientific certainty shall not be used as a reason for postponing cost-effective measures to prevent environmental degradation[77]

Earth Summit 2002

The World Summit on Sustainable Development,[78] or Earth Summit 2002 took place in Johannesburg, South Africa, from 26 August to 6 September 2002. This conference is also known as Rio +10.

It was convened to discuss sustainable development by the United Nations.[79] The Johannesburg Declaration was the main outcome of the Summit.[80]

---

[76] http://research.un.org/en/docs/environment/conferences
[77] www.unep.org/Documents.Multilingual/Default.asp?DocumentID=78&ArticleID=1163
[78] http://www.earthsummit2002.org/
[79] General Assembly resolution 55/199 of 20 December 2000
[80] Johannesburg Declaration on Sustainable Development

The conference also reviewed the progress of the implementation of Agenda 21.

The United Nations Conference on Sustainable Development

The United Nations Conference[81] on Sustainable Development[82] (UNCSD), also known as Rio +20[83] was held in Rio de Janeiro, 20-22 June 2012. The Rio +20 was one of the largest event which has witnessed the huge gathering. The participants included 192 member states and NGO's.

The main focus of the event was based on two themes,
1) A Green economy in the context of sustainable development and poverty eradication.

2) The institutional framework for sustainable development.[84]

International treaties, Conventions, Conferences, Protocols helped in the development of legislation to protect the environment and framing policies to protect and improve the environment, preventing pollution, etc.

There are, however, some international agreements and regulatory principles, which form the basis for health care waste management rules at the national level.

---

[81] Called for by General Assembly resolution 66/197
[82] http://www.un.org/en/sustainablefuture/about.shtml
[83] http://www.undp.org/content/undp/en/home/presscenter/events/2012/June/rio-20-sustainable-development.html
[84] https://www.environment.gov.au/about-us/international/rio-20

1. The Brundtland Commission on Environment and Development, in its 1987 Report, Our Common Future[85] held that sustainable development is

"development that meets the needs of the present without compromising the ability of future generations to meet their own needs."[86]

The parameters of sustainable development are clarified in Agenda 21 and the Rio Declaration, both adopted at UNCED, and in subsequent international regional and national instruments.

Principle 4 of the Rio Declaration states[87]

"In order to achieve sustainable development, environmental protection shall constitute an integral part of the development process and cannot be considered in isolation from it."

Principle 25 states[88] that

"Peace, development and environmental protection are interdependent and indivisible."

---

[85] http://www.un-documents.net/our-common-future.pdf
[86] http://www.un-documents.net/ocf-02.htm
[87] http://www.un.org/documents/ga/conf151/aconf15126-1annex1.htm
[88] *ibid*

2. "Polluter Pays" Principle is an important principle which penalizes the wrong doer. It recognizes that the polluter should pay for any environmental damage created, and that the burden of proof in demonstrating that a particular technology, practice or product is safe should lie with the developer, not the general public.[89]

The first mention of the Principle at the international level is to be found in the 1972 Recommendation by the OECD Council on Guiding Principles concerning International Economic Aspects of Environmental Policies[90] where it stated that,

"The principle to be used for allocating costs of pollution prevention and control measures to encourage rational use of scarce environmental resources and to avoid distortions in international trade and investment is the so-called Polluter-Pays Principle."

"This principle means that the polluter should bear the expenses of carrying out the above-mentioned measures decided by public authorities to ensure that the environment is in an acceptable state[91]

---

[89] http://www.sustainable-environment.org.uk/Principles/Polluter_Pays.php
[90] http://www.oecd.org/trade/envtrade/39918312.pdf
[91] http://www.oecd.org/trade/envtrade/39918312.pdf

3. The precautionary principle is an integral principle of sustainable development that is development that meets the needs of the present without compromising the abilities of future generations to meet their needs.[92]

The Precautionary Principle[93] was incorporated into the 1992 Rio Declaration on Environment and Development, stating that,

"Where there are threats of serious or irreversible damage, lack of full scientific certainty shall not be used as a reason for postponing cost-effective measures to prevent environmental degradation".[94]

4. Principle 21 of the Stockholm Declaration recognizes the sovereign right of each state upon its natural resources, emphasizing that it is limited by the responsibility for tran-boundary harm. 1972 Stockholm Declaration Principle 21[95]

"States have, in accordance with the Charter of the United Nations and the principles of international law, the sovereign right to exploit their own resources pursuant to their own environmental policies, and the responsibility to ensure that activities within their jurisdiction or control do not cause damage to the environment of other States or of areas beyond the limits of national jurisdiction."

---

[92] http://www.eubios.info/UNESCO/precprin.pdf
[93] Principle 15
[94] http://www.gdrc.org/u-gov/precaution-7.html
[95] http://www.unep.org/Documents.Multilingual/Default.asp?documentid=97&articleid=1503

India is signatory to international conventions and treaty and has adopted various rules to deal with different types of waste. Biomedical waste has been dealt under Biomedical Wastes (Management and Handling) Rules, 1998. The following are legislation along with the kind of waste management.

a) The Hazardous Wastes (Management, Handling and Tran boundary Movement) Rules, 2008.[96]

(b) Waste-water and exhaust gases as covered under the provisions of the Water (Prevention and Control of Pollution) Act, 1974 (6 of 1974)[19] and the Air (Prevention and Control of Pollution) Act, 1981 (14 of 1981)[97]

(c) Wastes arising out of the operation from ships beyond five kilometers of the relevant baseline as covered under the provisions of the Merchant Shipping Act, 1958 (44 of 1958)[98] and the rules made thereunder.

(d) Radio-active wastes as covered under the provisions of the Atomic Energy Act, 1962 (33 of 1962)[99] and the rules made thereunder.

---

[96] http://mpcb.gov.in/hazardous/pdf/HWRulesFinalNoti240908.pdf
[97] www.moef.nic.in/legis/air/air1.html
[98] labour.gov.in/.../ActsandRules/...and.../TheMerchantShippingAct1958.p
[99] dae.nic.in/?q=node/153

(e) Biomedical wastes covered under the Biomedical Wastes (Management and Handling) Rules, 1998[100] made under the Act; and

(f) Wastes covered under the Municipal Solid Wastes (Management and Handling) Rules, 2000[101] made under the Act;

---

[100] envfor.nic.in/legis/hsm/biomed.html
[101] www.moef.nic.in/legis/hsm/mswmhr.html

8

Judicial Trend on Waste Management and Environment

The Constitution (Forty Second Amendment) Act 1976[102] explicitly incorporated environmental protection and improvement as part of State policy through the insertion of Article 48A.[103]

Article 51A (g)[104] imposes a similar responsibility on every citizen "to protect and improve the natural environment including forests, lakes, rivers, and wildlife and to have compassion for all living creatures."

Article 48A provides for protection and improvement of the environment and safeguarding of forests and wildlife.

"The State shall endeavor to protect and improve the environment and to safeguard the forests and wild life of the country"

---

[102] http://indiacode.nic.in/coiweb/amend/amend42.htm
[103] http://www.constitution.org/cons/india/p04048a.html
[104] http://www.constitution.org/cons/india/p4a51a.html

Article 21[105] of the Constitution of India, which guarantees 'right to life', Protection of life and personal liberty states,

"No person shall be deprived of his life or personal liberty except according to procedure established by law" and safe and healthy environment is a part of article 21.

Rural Litigation and Entitlement Kendra v. State of U.P.[106] was one of the earliest cases where the Supreme Court dealt with issues relating to the environment and ecological balance.

The Supreme Court in the **CharanLal Sahu case.**[107] Similarly, in **Subash Kumar case,**[108] the Court observed that 'right to life guaranteed by article 21 includes the right of enjoyment of pollution-free water and air for full enjoyment of life.' Through this case, the Court recognized the right to a wholesome environment as part of the fundamental right to life.

This case also indicated that the municipalities and a large number of other concerned governmental agencies could no longer rest content with unimplemented measures for the abatement and prevention of pollution. They may be compelled to take positive measures to improve the environment.

---

[105] http://www.constitution.org/cons/india/p03021.html
[106] 1985 AIR 652, 1985 SCR (3) 169
[107] Charan Lal Sahu v. Union of India AIR 1990 SC 1480

In **M.C. Mehta Vs. Union of India**[109] and others a Three Judges Bench of Supreme Court held that Article 39 (e), 47 and 48-A by themselves and collectively cast a duty on the State to secure the health of the people, improve public health and protect and improve the environment.

"Articles 39 (e), 47 and 48A by themselves and collectively cast a duty on the State to secure the health of the people, improve public health and protect and improve the environment. It was by reason of the lack of effort on the part of the enforcement gencies, notwithstanding adequate laws being in place, that this Court has been concerned with the state of air pollution in the capital of this country. Lack of concern or effort on the part of various governmental agencies had resulted in spiralling pollution levels."

In **M.C. Mehta v Union of India (UOI) and Ors.,** the Apex Court held that there has been accelerated degradation of the environment and it reiterated that the right to live is a fundamental right under Article 21 of the Constitution and it includes the right of enjoyment of pollution free air for the enjoyment of life.

It was further observed that the most vital necessities such as air, water and soil having regard to the right to life under Article 21, cannot be permitted to be misused and polluted so as to reduce the quality of life of others

---

[108] Subhash Kumar v. State of Bihar, AIR 1991 SC 420

The judgement delivered by Justice V.R. Krishna Iyer in **Ratlam Municipality Case**[110] in 1980 has viewed the concept of public nuisance in an environmental sense. In this case, the Supreme Court dismissed the argument of the Ratlam Municipality that it could not perform the statutory duties due to financial inability.

The Court ordered the Municipality to provide the basic civic facilities to the public without making lame excuses. This Judgement became an eye opener for the public-spirited individuals and encouraged them to file litigations to solve local environmental issues.

This reformed the whole system and a number of cases have been filed before different courts seeking remedies against environmental pollution.

"Public nuisance, because of pollutants being discharged by big factories to the detriment of the poorer sections, is a challenge to the social justice component of the rule of law. Likewise, the grievous failure of local authorities to provide the basic amenity of public conveniences drives the miserable slum-dwellers to ease in the streets, on the sly for a time, and openly thereafter, because under nature's pressure, bashfulness becomes a luxury and dignity a difficult art.

---

[109] 2002 (2) SCR 963
[110] 1980 AIR 1622, 1981 SCR (1)97

A responsible municipal council constituted for the precise purpose of preserving public health and providing better finances cannot run away from its principal duty by pleading financial inability. Decency and dignity are non-negotiable facets of human rights and are a first charge on local self-governing bodies. Similarly, providing drainage systems- not pompous and attractive, but in working condition and sufficient to meet the needs of the people- cannot be evaded if the municipality is to justify its existence. A bare study of the statutory provisions makes this position clear."

In **Vellore Citizens Welfare Forum case,**[111] the Supreme Court was approached by the petitioner to issue directions against the tannery pollution caused by the discharge of untreated effluents in the Vellore area in Tamilnadu. The untreated effluents affected the agricultural lands, groundwater and health of the local people.

The Court delivered a landmark judgment in this case and directed the tanneries to set up effluent treatment plants. The tanneries, which failed to establish effluent treatment plants, were closed in the interest of the public.

In a landmark judgment on medical waste management, the Supreme Court in connection with safe disposal of hospital waste ordered that,

---

[111] AIR1996 SC 2715, (1996) 5 SCC 647

(a) All hospitals with 50 beds and above should install either their own incinerator or an equally effective alternative method before 30th November 1996.

(b) The incinerator or the alternative method should be installed with a necessary pollution control mechanism conforming to the standard laid down by the Central Pollution Control Board (CPCB).

(c) Hazardous medical waste should be segregated at source and disinfected before final disposal.

In this background in persuasion to the directive of The Court, the Ministry of Environment and Forests, Government of India notified the BioMedical Waste (management and Handling) Rule on 27th July 1998; under the provision of the Environment Protection Act 1986. Accordingly, all the hospitals in the public and private sector are now bound to follow these rules.

It regulated the disposal of biomedical wastes and lays down the procedures for collection, treatment and disposal and standards to be complied with.

These rules apply to all persons, who generate, collect, receive, store, transport, and treat or handle biomedical wastes in any form. Biomedical wastes mean any waste, which is generated during the diagnosis, treatment or immunization of human beings or animals or in research activities etc.[112]

---

[112] AIR 1996 SC 2969, (1996)2 SCC 594, [1996]3 SCR 80

9

Biomedical waste law worldwide

United kingdom

In the UK there is specific legislation to deal with hazardous clinical waste.

All clinical waste handling and disposal procedures comply with the following regulations:

The Environmental Protection Act 1990 (including the Duty of Care Regulations)[113]

The Controlled Waste Regulations 2012[114]

The Hazardous Waste Directive 2011[115]

The Carriage of Dangerous Goods Regulations[116]

---

[113] http://www.legislation.gov.uk/ukpga/1990/43/contents
[114] http://www.legislation.gov.uk/uksi/2012/811/pdfs/uksi_20120811_en.pdf
[115] https://www.gov.uk/waste-legislation-and-regulations
[116] http://www.hse.gov.uk/cdg/

The main legislation governing clinical waste disposal is The Environmental Protection Act 1990. This stipulates that all producers of waste have a Duty of Care to ensure the correct and proper management of waste is performed and states that it is unlawful to deposit, recover or dispose of controlled clinical waste without a waste management licence, or in a way that causes pollution of the environment or harm to human health.[117]

Section 34 (1) imposes a duty on

"any person who imports, produces, carries, keeps, treats or disposes of controlled waste or, as a broker, has control of such waste, to take all such measures applicable to him in that capacity as are reasonable in the circumstances"

The statutory duty of care applies to everyone in the waste management chain. It requires producers and others who are involved in the management of the waste to prevent its escape, and to take all reasonable measures to ensure that the waste is dealt with appropriately from the point of production to the point of final disposal.[118]

This is enforced through the "polluter pays principle", making producers of waste responsible for its management and disposal.

---

[117] http://www.nature.com/articles/bdjteam201438
[118] https://www.isopharm.co.uk/dental/clinical-waste

The department of health had issued Health Technical Memorandum (HTM) 07-01 guidelines[119] for those involved in the management and disposal of healthcare waste. It provides guidance on the secure and legally compliant management of clinical waste.

Clinical waste is defined as:

"... any waste which consists wholly or partly of human or animal tissue, blood or other body fluids, excretions, drugs or other pharmaceutical products, swabs or dressings, syringes, needles or other sharp instruments, being waste which unless rendered safe may prove hazardous to any person coming into contact with it; and b. any other waste arising from medical, nursing, dental, veterinary, pharmaceutical or similar practice, investigation, treatment, care, teaching or research, or the collection of blood for transfusion, being waste which may cause infection to any person coming into contact with it."

Clinical waste can be divided into three broad groups of materials:
 a) Any healthcare waste which poses a risk of infection
 b) Certain healthcare wastes which pose a chemical hazard
 c) Medicines and medicinally-contaminated waste containing a pharmaceutically active agent

United States of America
The Medical Waste Tracking Act (MWTA) of 1988.[120]

---

[119] https://www.gov.uk/government/publications/guidance-on-the-safe-management-of-healthcare-waste
[120] http://www.epa.gov/osw/nonhaz/industrial/medical/tracking.htm

The Medical Waste tracking Act of 1988 defines medical waste as *"any solid waste that is generated in the diagnosis, treatment, or immunization of human beings or animals, in research pertaining thereto, or in the production or testing of biologicals."*

The Medical Waste Tracking Act (MWTA) was enacted in 1988. The Act amended the Solid Waste Disposal Act. It defined medical waste and established which medical wastes would be subject to program regulations. The MWTA required management standards for segregation, packaging, labeling and marking, and storage of the medical waste.[121]

The Act also established record keeping requirements and penalties that could be imposed for mismanagement. The MWTA required the EPA to examine various treatment technologies such as incinerators and autoclaves, microwave units and various chemical and mechanical systems for their ability to reduce the disease causing potential of medical waste.[122]

The features of the legislation are following,

a) Defined medical waste and established which medical wastes would be subject to program regulations.

---

[121] http://www.lehman.edu/administration/environmental-health-safety/regulated-medical-waste.php
[122] http://environmentallaw.uslegal.com/specific-issues/medical-waste/

b) Established a cradle-to-grave tracking system utilizing a generator initiated tracking form.

c) Required management standards for segregation, packaging, labeling and marking, and storage of the medical waste.

d) Established record keeping requirements and penalties that could be imposed for mismanagement.

In addition to on-site treatment or pickup by a biomedical waste disposal firm for off-site treatment, a mail-back disposal option exists in the United States. In mail-back biomedical waste disposal, the waste is shipped through the U.S. postal service.[123]

Medical waste disposal is primarily regulated at the state level. However, certain medical waste is disposed according to federal law. The health care facilities, like hospitals, physician's offices, dental practices and veterinary hospitals, etc. Many of these wastes are regulated at the state and local level and some of them are governed by federal regulations.

---

[123] http://www.wow.com/wiki/Medical_waste

States develop regulations for office and municipal type waste, whereas the federal government develops regulations for hazardous waste. State regulations generally cover potentially infectious medical waste, also referred as regulated medical waste.[124]

Canada

In Canada extensive guidelines exist for the management of certain types of waste for e.g., the Canadian Council of Ministers of the Environment (CCME) has *Guidelines for the Management of Biomedical Waste in Canada.*[125]

Biomedical waste can be defined as waste generated in human and animal health care facilities, medical or veterinary research and training facilities, clinical testing or research laboratories, as well as vaccine production facilities.

CCME has also developed Canada-wide guidelines for defining, handling, treating, and disposing of biomedical waste. The intent of these guidelines is to promote uniform practices and set minimum standards for managing biomedical waste in Canada.[126]

It defines biomedical Waste defines as,

---

[124] http://lamprecycling.veoliaes.com/newsletter/June2012/5
[125] http://www.ccme.ca/files/Resources/waste/pn_1060_e.pdf
[126] http://canadianbiosafetystandards.collaboration.gc.ca/cbh-gcb/ch16-20-eng.php

a) Human Anatomical Waste This consists of human tissues, organs, and body parts, but does not include teeth, hair, and nails.

b) Animal Waste This consists of all animal tissues, organs, body parts, carcasses, bedding, fluid blood and blood products, items saturated or dripping with blood, body fluids contaminated with blood, and body fluids removed for diagnosis or removed during surgery, treatment or autopsy, unless a trained person has certified that the waste does not contain the viruses and agents listed in Risk Group 4 (see table 1). This excludes teeth, hair, nails, hooves, and feathers.

c) Microbiology Laboratory Waste
This consists of Laboratory cultures, stocks or specimens of microorganisms, live or attenuated vaccines, human or animal cell cultures used in research, and laboratory material that has come into contact with any of these.

d) Human Blood and Body Fluid waste
This consists of human fluid blood and blood products, items saturated or dripping with blood, body fluids contaminated with blood, and body fluids removed for diagnosis during surgery, treatment or autopsy. This does not include urine or feces.

e) Waste Sharps
Waste sharps are clinical and laboratory materials consisting of needles, syringes, blades, or laboratory glass capable of causing punctures or cuts.

f) Cytotoxic Waste

The term is commonly used to refer to the pharmaceuticals used in treating cancer, e.g., antineoplastics or chemotherapy agents

South Australia

Environment Protection (Waste to Resources) Policy 2010 under the Environment Protection Act 1993[127] provides waste management including biomedical waste.

It states that the objective of this policy is to achieve sustainable waste management by applying the waste management hierarchy consistently with the principles of ecologically sustainable development.

The medical waste means waste consisting of —
(a) Medical sharps; or
(b) Human tissue, bone, organ, body part or fetus; or
(c) A vessel, bag or tube containing a liquid body substance; or
(d) An animal carcass discarded in the course of veterinary research or medical practice or research; or

   (e) a specimen or culture discarded in the course of medical, dental or veterinary practice or research and any material that has come into contact with such a specimen or culture; or

---

[127] http://www.legislation.sa.gov.au/LZ/C/POL/ENVIRONMENT%20PROTECTION%20%28WASTE%20TO%20RESOURCES%29%20POLICY%202010/CURRENT/2010.-.UN.PDF

(f) any other article or matter that is discarded in the course of medical, dental or veterinary practice or research and that poses a significant risk to the health of a person who comes into contact with it;

Further the Environment Protection (Waste to Resources) Policy 2010[128] under division 2—Medical waste, 16 - *Collection and transport of medical waste provides* that

(1) Medical waste produced in the course of a prescribed activity must, as soon as is reasonably practicable after its production, be placed in a prescribed container and—

(a) Collected for disposal by—
(i) a licensed waste transporter authorised to collect and transport medical waste; or
(ii) a council; or
(b) Transported by a person employed or engaged in the business producing the waste directly to—
(i) a licensed depot at which medical waste may be received pursuant to the licence; or
(ii) a hospital.

---

[128]https://www.legislation.sa.gov.au/LZ/C/POL/ENVIRONMENT%20PROTECTION%20(WASTE%20TO%20RESOURCES)%20POLICY%202010/CURRENT/2010.-.UN.PDF

Hong Kong

The Waste Disposal (Amendment) Ordinance 2006[129] enacted on 7 April 2006 to implement the Clinical Waste Control Scheme, through waste disposal (clinical waste) (general) regulation.

The main features of the legislature are following,

(a) Requiring clinical waste producers to properly manage their clinical waste by segregating those wastes from other municipal solid waste and consigning the clinical waste to licensed waste collectors for disposal;

(b) Establishing a statutory licensing requirement for clinical waste collectors;

(c) Promulgating to the parties concerned two sets of Code of Practice ("CoP") to provide guidance on the handling and management of clinical waste;

(d) Setting up a trip ticket system to track clinical waste from source to disposal facility;

(e) Designating the Chemical Waste Treatment Centre ("CWTC") as the Government facility to treat clinical waste; and

(f) Levying a charge on the clinical waste to be disposed of at the CWTC.[130]

---

[129] http://www.epd.gov.hk/epd/clinicalwaste/nonflash/english/downloads/files/wd_a_ordinance_2006_gazetted_e.pdf

[130] http://www.legco.gov.hk/yr09-10/english/subleg/brief/83_84_brf.pdf

This Regulation provides for the control and regulation of the disposal and delivery of clinical waste. Some important feature of the regulation are following,

1. Section 1 provides for the commencement of the Regulation.

2. Section 2 sets out the definitions necessary for the interpretation of the Regulation.

3. Sections 3 and 4 impose a duty to dispose of clinical waste properly and provide for the means by which clinical waste may be properly disposed of.

4. Section 5 requires a licensed waste collector to deliver the clinical waste that the licensed waste collector has collected to a reception point (as defined in section 2) within 24 hours or, where the Director of Environmental Protection ("the Director") by a direction requires the licensed waste collector to deliver any clinical waste collected by the licensed waste collector to a specified reception point within a specified period, to deliver the clinical waste to that reception point within that period.

5. Section 6 empowers the Director to require removal of clinical waste.

6. Section 7 requires a person handling clinical waste to take precautions to prevent danger to public health or safety, pollution to the environment and nuisance to the neighboring area.

7. Section 8 provides for the circumstances under which a waste disposal license may be granted.

8. Section 9 provides for the authorization for using land or premises used for certain purposes (such as a dental, medical, nursing or veterinary practice) as a collection point.

9. Section 10 provides for the Director's power to authorize a person to collect or remove clinical waste without a waste collection license. That section also provides for the Director's power to authorize a person to use specified land or premises for the disposal of clinical waste without a waste disposal license.[131]

---

[131] http://www.legco.gov.hk/yr09-10/english/subleg/brief/83_84_brf.pdf

10

Biomedical Waste Management - A Study of Satara City

In India it is estimated that the quantum of waste generated is around 1-2 kg per bed per day in a hospital and 600 gm per day, per bed in a general practitioner's clinic.[132] The World health organization has reported that around 15% of the waste generated from health care activities may be infectious, toxic or radioactive and the remaining 85% is non hazardous waste.[133]

The report further says that health care waste can infect patients, health workers and the general public as it contains potentially harmful microorganisms.[134]

The waste generated from health care units must be disposed efficiently otherwise it can cause infection to the public at large. According to the World Health Organization health care waste have both health and environment risk.

---

[132] http://www.medwasteind.org/random.asp
[133] http://www.who.int/mediacentre/factsheets/fs253/en/
[134] *ibid*

According to it an infected needle stick can cause risk of becoming infected with HBV, HCV and HIV. Similarly, it can also cause serious damage to the environment, including drinking water when not disposed properly.[135]

Objectives

1) To evaluate legal provisions related to collection, disposal and management of biomedical waste in India and abroad.

2) To review, analysis and study literature, data with regard to biomedical waste management and practices in Satara city.

3) To evaluate the implementation of legal rules and regulation in Satara City by the health care establishment, especially in relation to BioMedical Waste (Management and Handling) Rules, 1998.

4) To assess the current situation in the city of the Satara city with regard to bio waste generation, collection, management and disposal of biomedical waste.

5) To carry out survey of health care establishments in the Satara city to assess the existing practices of collection, segregation, storage, transportation and disposal of biomedical waste.

6) To monitor common biomedical waste treatment plant and disposal facility located at Songoan, JakatWadi, Satara used for disposal of biomedical waste generated by the Satara city and nearby locations.

7) To identify and study areas requiring consideration in the implementation of biomedical facility in Satara city.

---

[135] http://www.who.int/mediacentre/factsheets/fs253/en/

8) To propose suggestions for the improvement in the implementation of biomedical rules in Satara city.

9) To arrive at the concluding remark.

Hypothesis

The following hypotheses were formulated and studied to ascertain the issues in the biomedical waste disposal system in Satara City.

H1. The practices of biomedical waste management and disposal in Satara are not in line with the rules enacted by the Central Government and amended from time to time.

H2. The awareness of biomedical waste rules is lacking amongst health care establishments in Satara City.

H3. The Common biomedical disposal facility plays a vital role in biomedical waste management.

Methodology

Since the study involves interdisciplinary issues, doctoral as well as non doctoral methods of study will be undertaken.

Universe of study

The study will be conducted in Satara city, hence it is limited to, all health care establishments within the boundaries of the Satara Municipal Council. The Satara Municipal Corporation is divided into 39 wards (Prabhag) for governance and representation.

As of 2011 India census, Satara had a population of 120,079; males constituted 52% of the population and females 48%. Satara City has an average literacy rate of 80%, higher than the national average of 74%: male literacy is 84%, and female literacy is 76%. In Satara City, 10% of the population are under 6 years of age. Marathi is the native and widely spoken languages. English, Kannada, Gujarati is also spoken. Like other large cities Satara city is divided into three parts urban area, Suburban areas, Industrial area. Suburban areas include SadarBazaar, Shahupuri,Shahunagar,Karanje,Godoli,Kodoli,Krishnanagar,Sangamnagar,Saidapur,Sangammahuli,Kshetramahuli,Vadhe,Kondave,Khed,Jakatwadi.

Out of these only Sadar bazaar is under municipal boundaries rest all are out of municipal boundaries. The area of major population is still out of municipal boundaries and it is under proposal to take it under municipal boundaries. The large number of the health care establishment is located in Sadar bazaar including the Government Civil Hospital.

Sample and Sampling

Health care establishment, especially hospitals in Satara City would be selected randomly by applying the simple random sampling method. This will constitute the sample for the study. Hence the total sample size of the study would be around 40%

Methods of data collection

Questionnaire, Interview and observation techniques will be used for collection of data. A questionnaire sheet shall a given to selected hospitals.

Few in depth case studies will be conducted to collect detailed information about implementation of legal norms and difficulties if any in their compliance.

A) Interview method with persons most knowledgeable about biomedical waste management disposal in hospitals facility.

b) On-site observations of biomedical waste management and handling practices at major hospitals and health care provider facilities.

c) Review of available reports/manuals on biomedical waste management by visit to various pollution control board authorities.

d) Review of available and existing biomedical waste management laws and legislation

e) Observation of biomedical waste treatment and disposal sites at Satara.

Tools of Data Collection

For accomplishing the above objectives, both primary and secondary data are collected. Primary data will be collected, by administering an interview schedule directly with the respondents.

Secondary sources of data collection will include reports published by State and Central government, Municipal reports, books, journals and periodicals.

Analysis of Data

The collected has been analyzed by using SPSS windows based version. The intellectual reasoning has been provided where ever necessary.

11

Results and Analysis

Based on the review of the literature and conceptual framework the following hypothesis were formulated and analyzed in the background of data collected.

The following hypotheses were formulated to ascertain the issues in the biomedical disposal system.

H1 The practices of biomedical waste management and disposal in Sataraare not in line with the rules enacted by the Government and amended from time to time.

H2 The awareness of biomedical waste rules is lacking amongst Health Care Establishments.

H3 Common biomedical disposal facility provides a vital role in Bio Medical Waste Management.

As part of data collection, responses were taken from doctors and supervisor of common biomedical waste disposal facility. The questions asked and responses collected are presented in the form of following graphs.

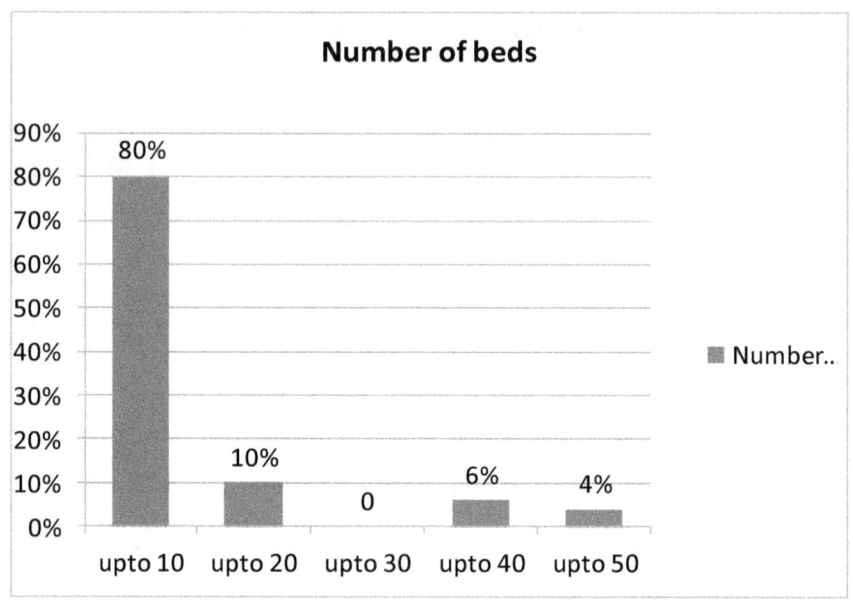

Health Care Establishments are the major generators of the biomedical medical waste. The Health Care Establishments are classified into two categories: Bedded HCEs i.e. Hospitals/ Nursing Homes with Bed Facility and Non-bedded HCEs.

The above charts show that major HCE in the Satara city is a small establishment in terms of number of beds. The 80% of HCE has a bed capacity only up to ten.

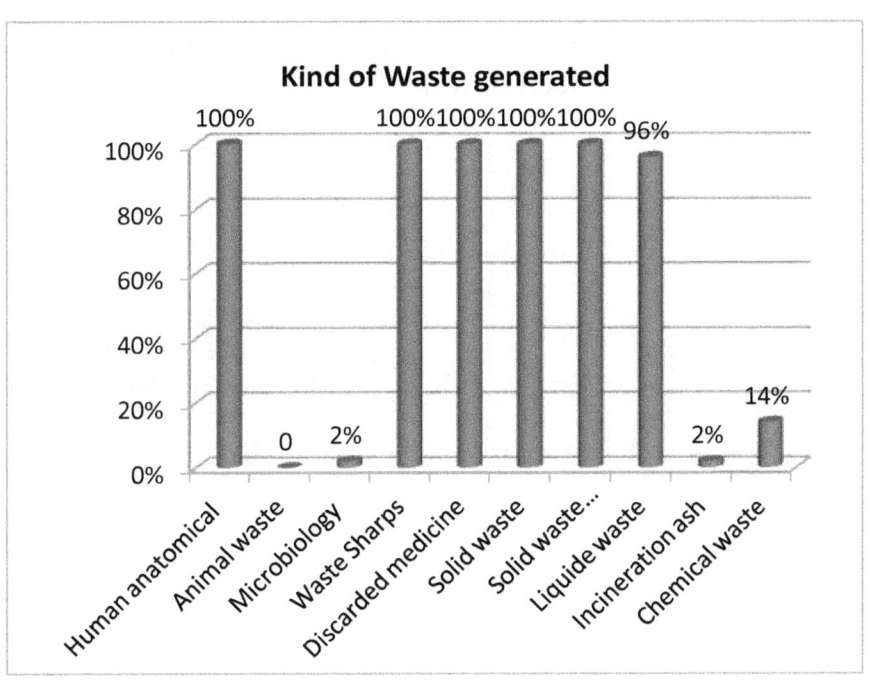

The health care establishment generates different types of biomedical wastes. The heavily generated biomedical wastes are human anatomical, waste sharps, discarded medicine, solid waste items like contaminated with blood, solid waste like disposable items like tubing, liquid waste.

In the study animal waste was nil and the generation of microbiological waste/biotechnology waste and incineration waste was least in terms of generation of waste.

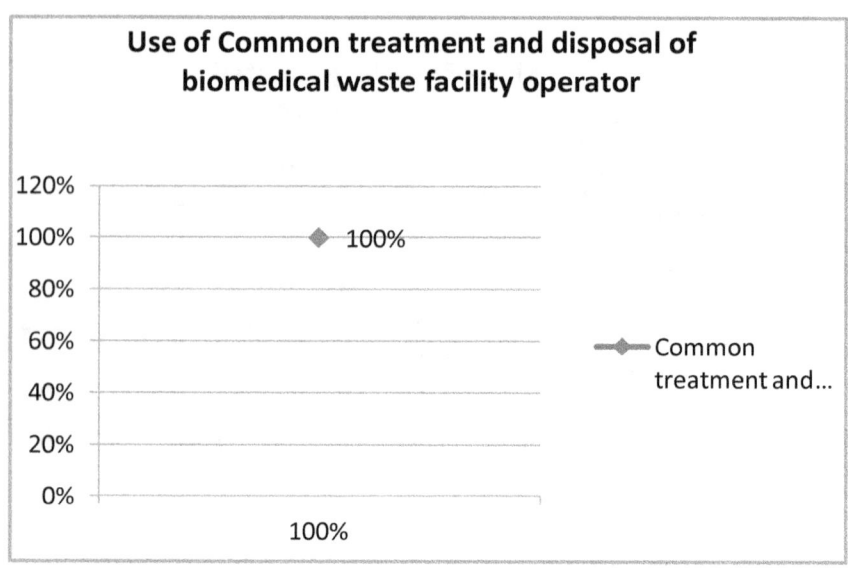

The study showed that 100% of HCE are using common treatment and disposal of biomedical waste facility operator service for disposal of biomedical waste.

The use of Common treatment plant provides specialized services to HCE who have to pay for the operators according the quantum of waste generated.

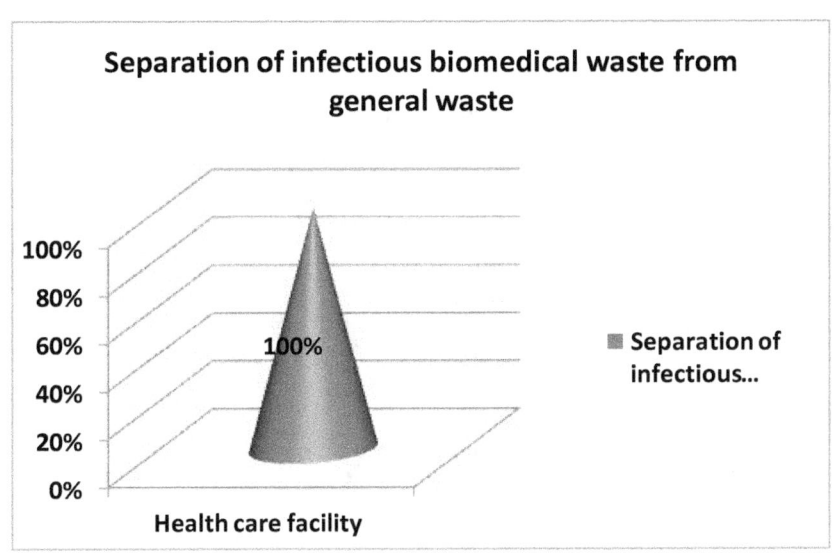

In the study it showed that all the HCE separates infectious biomedical wastes from general waste. This is commendable and it shows the awareness of contagious diseases and proper management of biomedical waste.

The bio-medical waste is segregated into container/ bags according to rules provided under rule 6 of the Biomedical Waste (Management and handing) Rules, 1998 and are not mixed with other wastes. It is not being mixed with municipal waste and is separated from other types of waste.

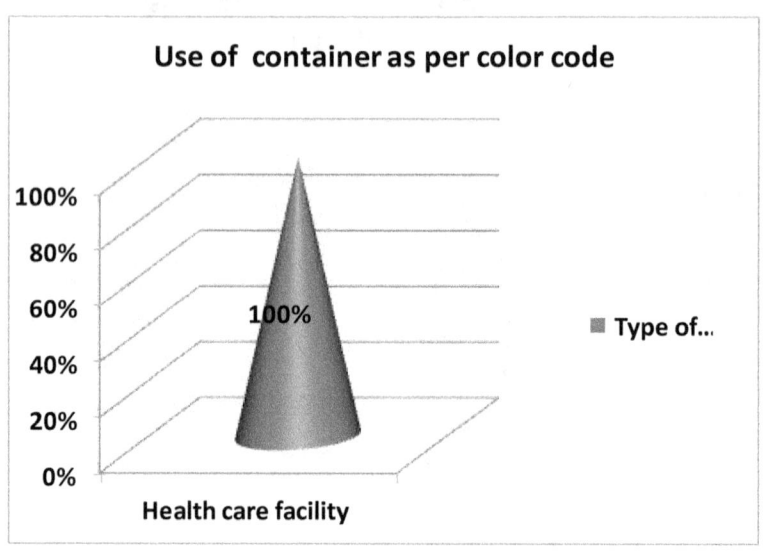

The bio-medical waste is segregated into container/ bags according to rules provided under rule 6 of the bio-medical rules. Biomedical waste is segregated into containers/bags at the point of generation in accordance with Schedule II, prior to its storage, transportation, treatment and disposal.

The segregation of bio-medical waste is an important element in the collection of bio-medical waste. The study showed that all health care establishments followed this rule stringently and biomedical waste is stored as per color code.

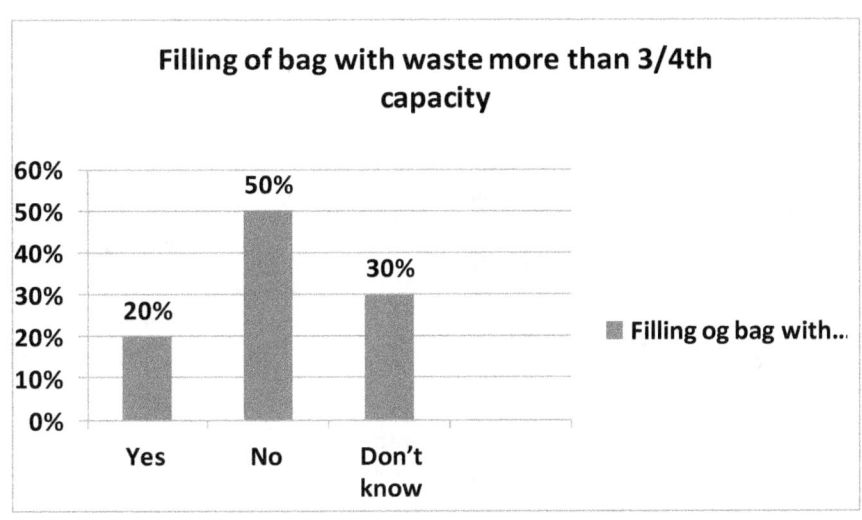

It is general practice that waste bags/container are filled fully thereby causing spillage. In response to the question that, whether bag/container are filled with waste for more than $3/4^{th}$ capacity, 50% responded no, 20% in yes and 30% said that they are not aware of this issue.

It is worth noting here that in the questionnaire a question was asked about the removal of biomedical waste for final disposal outside the hospital campus/clinic and majority stated that ward boy/nurse are responsible for final disposal.

Hence it can be presumed here that many health care establishments have a strong policy for final disposal and other issues related to it like filling of waste etc.

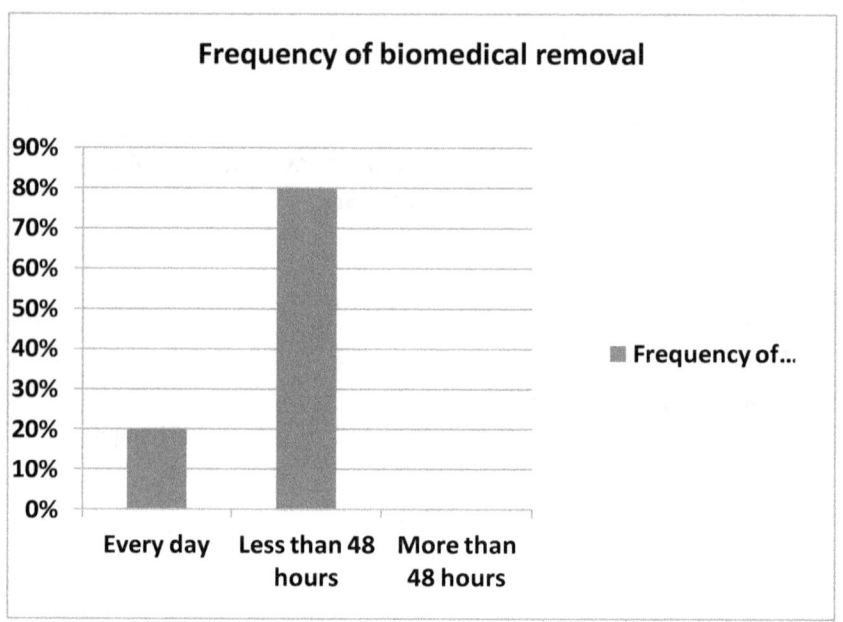

The bio-medical waste is segregated into container/ bags according to rules provided under rule 6 of the bio-medical rules. It provides that no untreated bio-medical waste shall be kept stored beyond a period of 48 hours. If for any reason it becomes necessary to store the waste beyond such period, the authorized person must take permission of the prescribed authority and have to take measures to ensure that the waste does not adversely affect human health and the environment.

The study showed that 20% of Health care establishment are sending their waste on the same day and 80% are sent within the 48 hrs. Hence it shows that prescribed rules are followed with regard to removal of biomedical waste.

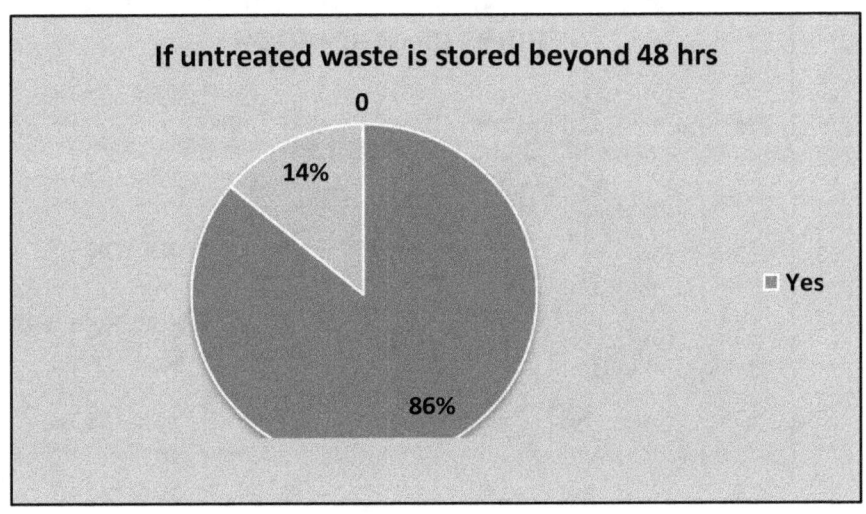

No untreated bio-medical waste shall be kept stored beyond a period of 48 hours. If for any reason it becomes necessary to store the waste beyond such period, the authorized person must take permission of the prescribed authority and have to take measures to ensure that the waste does not adversely affect human health and the environment. The health care establishment was asked whether they seek permission from the prescribed authority if in case the untreated waste is stored beyond 48hrs, 86% responded in negative and 14% responded that it is not applicable to them. When researcher inquired and discussed this issue with different health care establishment they accepted that in general, untreated waste is not stored beyond 48 hrs, however on rare occasions if it does happen, they don't seek permission. It shows that many health care establishments don't have clear guidelines regarding this issue. 14% responded that this condition is applicable to them as they have never faced such issue in the past.

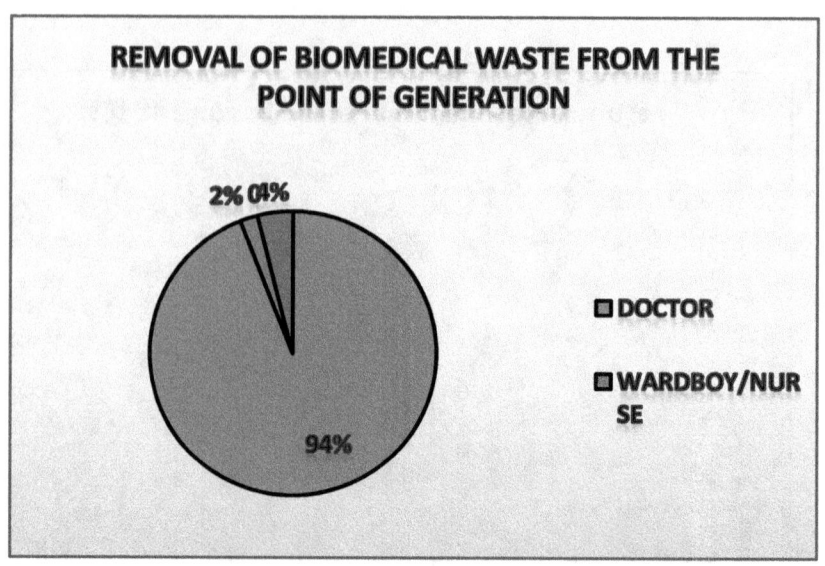

The rule 4 of the Biomedical Waste (Management and handing) Rules, 1998, impose duty of every occupier of an institution generating biomedical waste like a hospital, nursing home, clinic, dispensary, veterinary institution, animal house, pathological laboratory, blood bank etc., to take all steps to ensure that such waste is handled without any adverse effect to human health and the environment. It was found in 94% of the health care establishment, doctors were themselves were responsible of biomedical waste from point of generation for intermediate storage, 4% responded their sanitary staff and 2% responded that their ward boy/nurse are responsible for such practice. The practice of doctors removing biomedical waste is appreciable and shows that many health care establishments have a clear policy with regard to removal of biomedical waste.

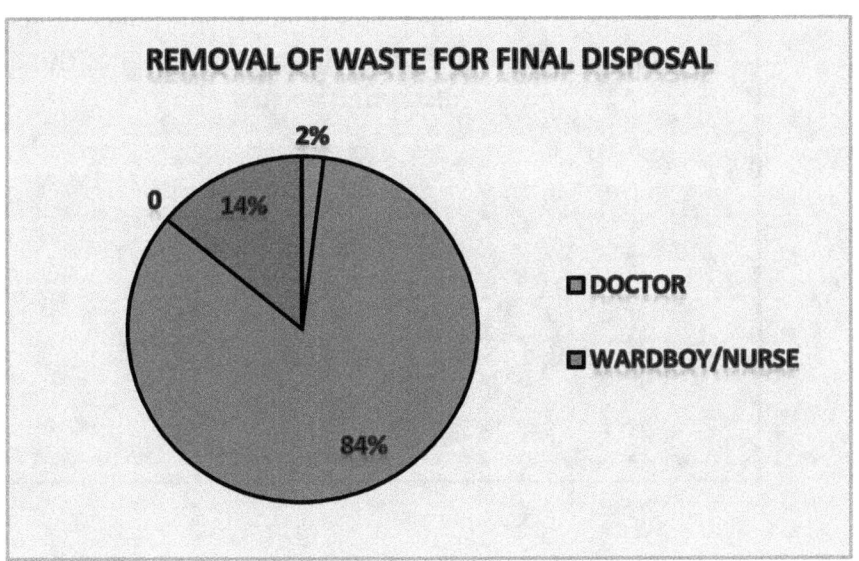

The removable of biomedical waste for final disposal outside the hospital campus/clinic were mainly through ward boy/nurse as 84% responded that in their establishment ward boy/nurse are responsible for final disposal.

The 14% stated that their sanitary does the task of final disposal and surprisingly 2% declared their doctors are removing biomedical waste for final disposal.

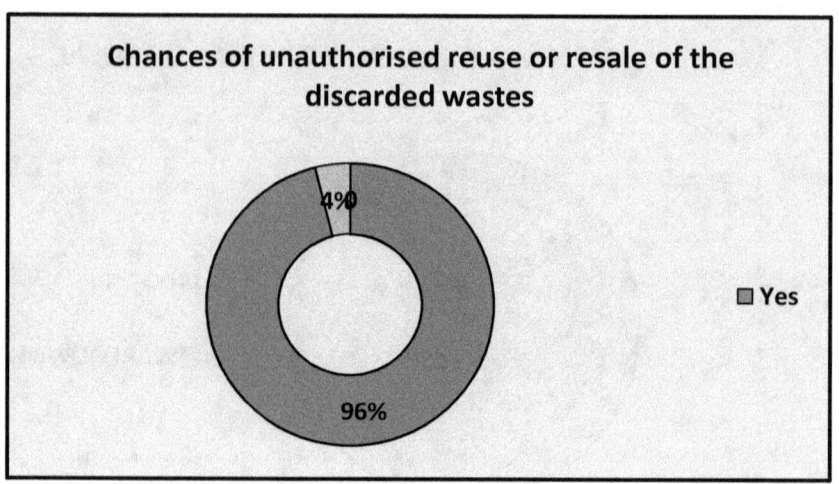

It is an important to take steps to prevent unauthorized use of discarded items or resale of discarded items. The discarded item usually carries contagious disease or infection which can spread disease to uninfected people.

96% health care responded that there is no chance of unauthorized use or resale of the discarded items by anyone within or outside the premises.

However, 4% responded were not sure whether discarded items can reuse or resold.

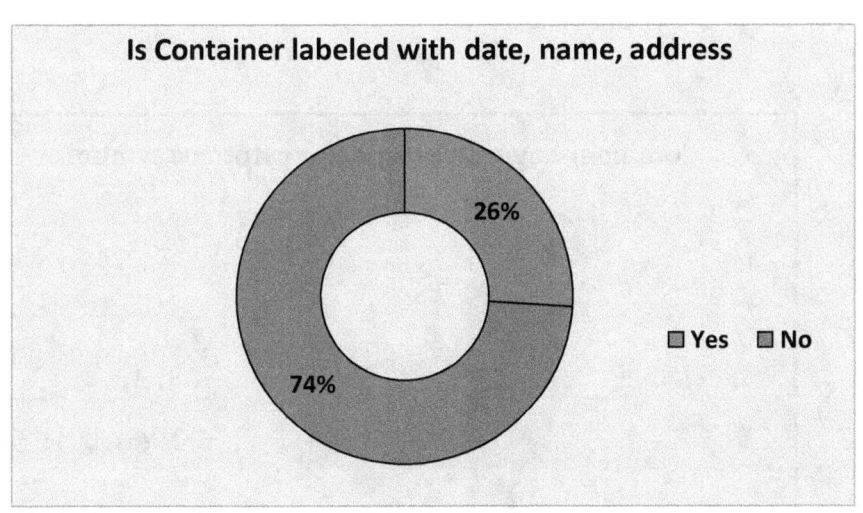

The rule 6 prescribes labeling of container according schedule III. It provides biomedical waste container/bags should have non-washable label displaying clearing the date, name, address, phone of the sender and receiver.

Only 26% responded in positive and 74% responded in negative showing that this norm is clearly flouted by many health care establishments.

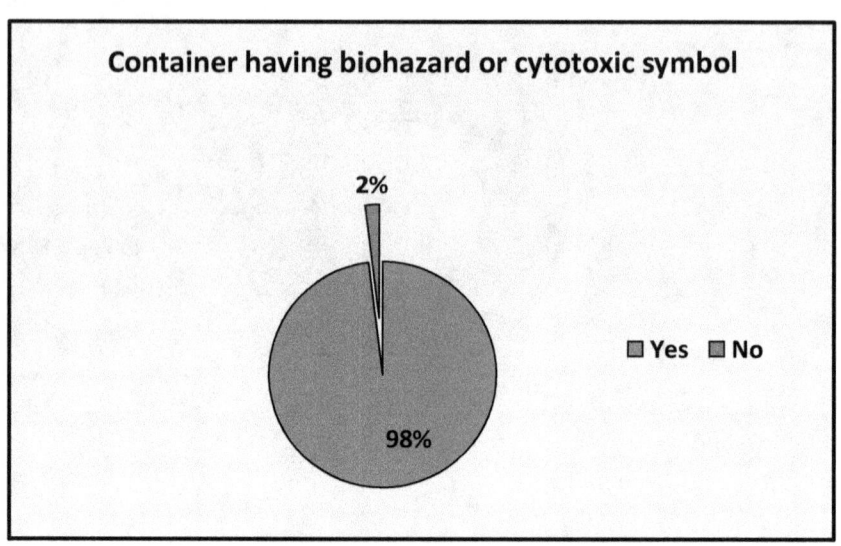

The schedule III of the rule provides for symbol or label for biomedical waste container/bags. It provides biomedical waste container/bags should have non-washable label and visibly display the biohazards or Cytotoxic symbol on it.

98% responded that their container/bags display such symbol. However, 2% said that their container/bags have no such symbol which is a violation of rules of biomedical waste disposal.

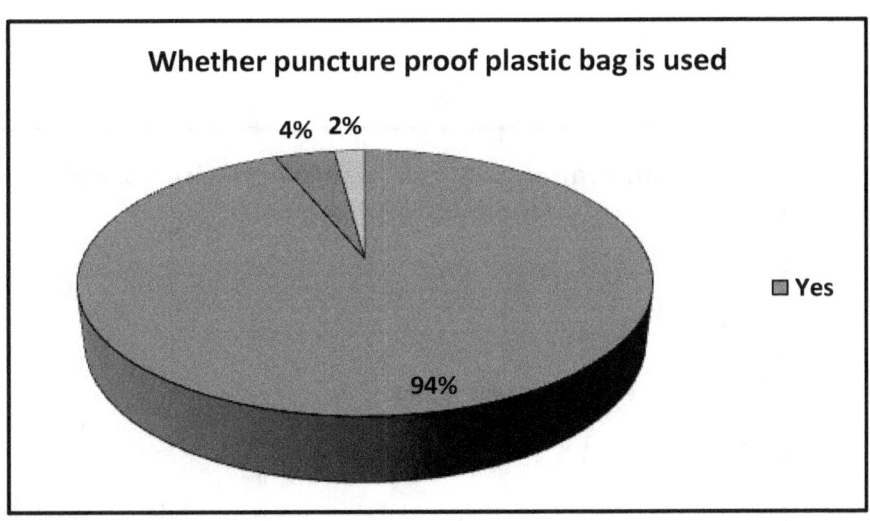

Schedule II provides for use of puncture proof bag for certain category of biomedical waste. 94% responded that they are using puncture proof bag for collection of sharps etc.

However, 4% said they are not using puncture proof bag and 2% said they don't know regarding this issue.

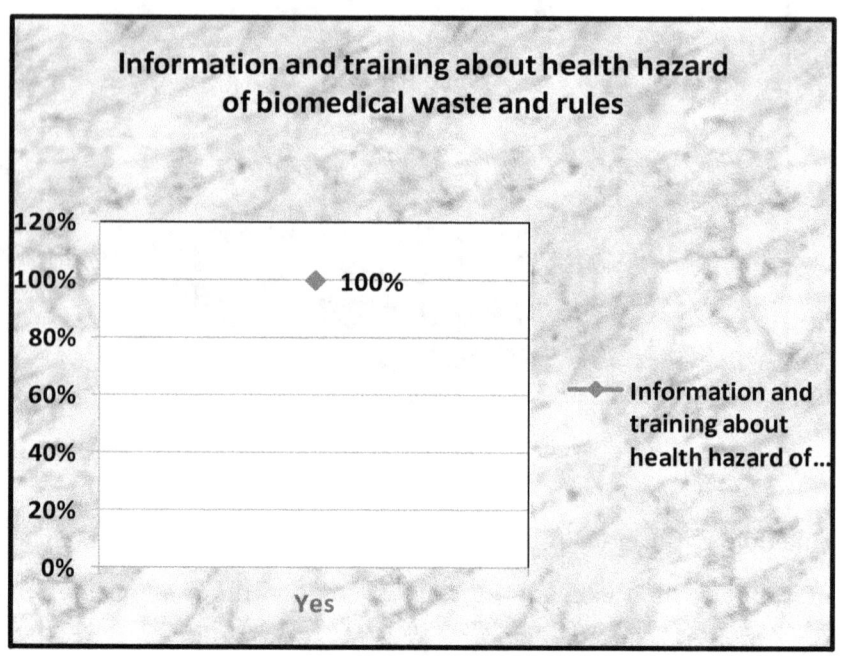

Information and training about the health hazards of biomedical waste and concerned rules for staff that are responsible for handling the biomedical waste is important for safe handling of biomedical waste. 100% responded in positive.

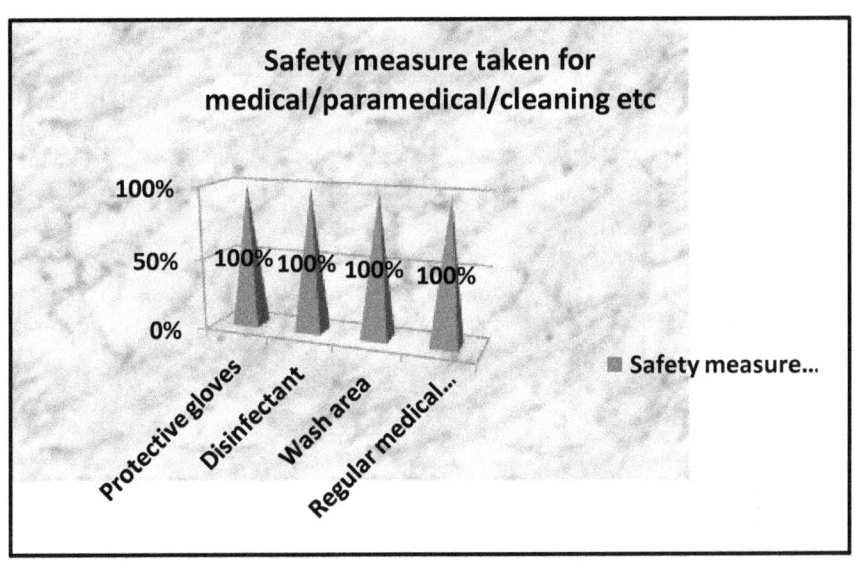

It is rightly said that precaution is better than cure. A question was asked on the safety measures which are taken for medical/paramedical staff who deal with biomedical waste.

The 100% health care establishment answered that they do they provide take safety measure like protective gloves, disinfectant and provide regular medical checkup etc.

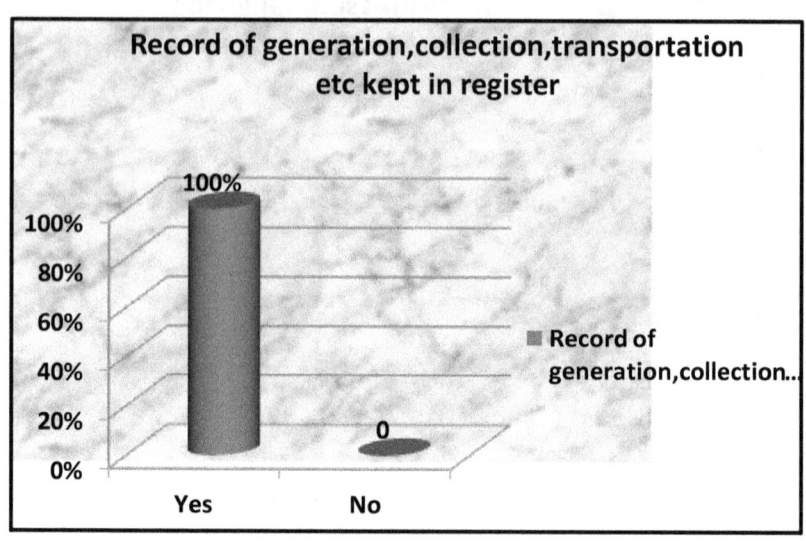

Every authorized person shall maintain records related to the generation, collection, reception, storage, transportation, treatment, disposal or any form of handling of bio-medical waste in accordance with the rules and any guidelines issued.

There were 100% positive responses. It was also found out during a visit and discussion that health care establishment were maintain register with regard to biomedical waste generation date, quantum of waste etc.

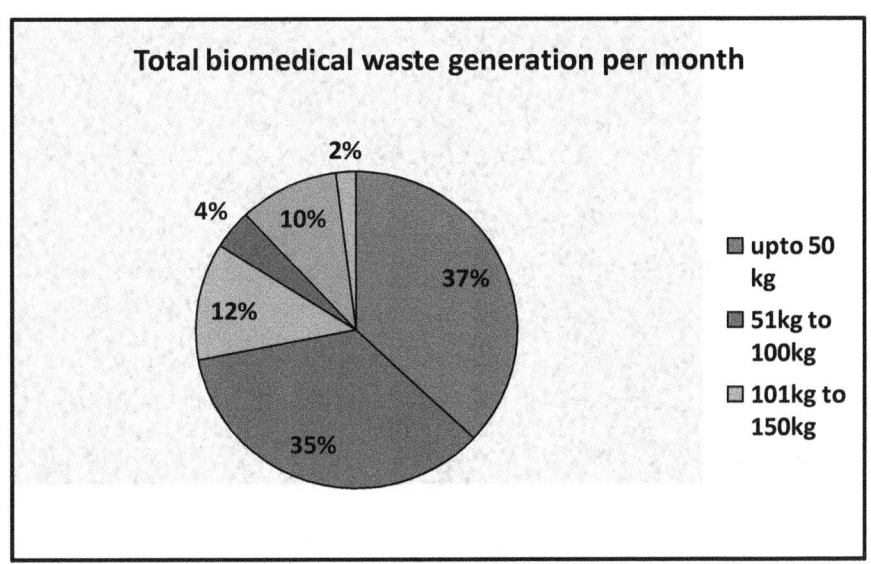

A question was asked in the questionnaire regarding the generation of biomedical waste per month by health care establishments. It was found that 37% of the health care establishment is generating approximately biomedical waste up to 50 kg per month and 35% up to 100 kg per month.

12% of the health care establishment were generating waste above 100 kg but less than 150 kg per month, 4% above 150 kg per month but less than 200 kg, 10% above 200 kg per month but less than 250 kg per month and 2% of health care establishment are generating waste above 250 kg but less than 300 kg per month.

12

Finding, Suggestions and Conclusion

The following hypothesis were formulated and tested to check the authenticity of the data collected.

Hypotheses

H1 The practices of biomedical waste disposal in Satara city, are not in line with the rules enacted by the Government and amended from time to time.

H2 The awareness about biomedical waste disposal rules is lacking amongst Health Care Establishments in Satara city.

H3 Common biomedical disposal facilities play a vital role in Bio Medical Waste Management.

Finding

On the basis of primary data, secondary data, interactions with the health care establishment and on site visit of common biomedical waste treatment facility have resulted in the revelation of following findings.

1) The health care establishments in Satara city are aware of the importance of proper handling and disposal of biomedical waste.

2) The majority of health care establishments in Satara city, are following the Biomedical Waste (Management and handing) Rules, 1998

3) The study has shown that 100% of HCE are using common biomedical waste treatment operator's services for disposal of biomedical waste.

4) The role of common biomedical waste treatment facility is very important in safe and prompt disposal of biomedical waste as per rules prescribed in this regard.CBMWTDF Nature in Need has Incinerator, shredder, Autoclaving machine, sterilization tank, Disinfectant Tank etc. and is substantially following the guidelines prescribed by Central Pollution Control board and Maharashtra Pollution Control Board from time to time regarding collection, transportation and disposal of biomedical waste.

5) It creditable to note that all health care establishments have adopted proper safety measures like protective gloves, disinfectant and provide regular medical checkup, etc. for medical/paramedical staffs who usually deal with biomedical waste.

6) It's worth noting that major health care establishments make it certain that discarded items are neither reused nor resold.

7) Health care establishment is providing regular information and training about the health hazards of biomedical waste and concerned rules for staff responsible for handling the biomedical waste.

8) However, norms were flouted regarding labels. Most of the health care establishments are failing to tag biomedical waste bag/container with date, name, address, phone of the sender and receiver etc. which are mandatory according to rules.

9) It has been observed that in most of the health care establishments, doctors are personally responsible for biomedical management.

10) It has been observed that the use of puncture proof bag for certain category of biomedical waste like sharps is mandatory, however, still few health care establishments are not using it thereby contravening the rules.

11) It has been observed that,health care establishments are taking training and awareness about biomedical waste issues and rules among its staff members.

12) From the site visit and supervision of Nature in Need and inspection of records and in discussion with health care establishments in Satara city, it can state that Common Biomedical Waste Treatment Facility (CBWTF) NATURE IN NEED plays an essential role in the safe Collection, Transportation, Treatment and disposal of the biomedical wastes.

Suggestions

1) The biomedical wastes must be segregated at the point of generation from non biomedical wastes properly according to Biomedical Waste (Management and handing) Rules, 1998. This is an important step to prevent contamination.

2) Currently health care establishments are not directly being monitored by the Government on the issue of biomedical waste. There should be surprise visits by the authorities to check the segregation and storage of biomedical waste. This will raise the seriousness of the issue.

3) Currently health care establishments are not writing policies with regard to biomedical management. There has to be proper policy documentation based on common guidelines issued by the appropriate authority.

4) It should be ensured that waste bags are filled up to only three fourth of its capacities and tied securely.

5) The health care establishment must have an awareness and training programs for its entire staff, including Doctors, nurses, ward boys, office and support staff as well as sanitary staff and guards and night watchmen.

6) It has come to notice that most of the health care establishment lacks separate room for storage for biomedical waste. The health care establishment should store, biomedical waste in a separate room to avoid contamination.

7) The waste must stored in leak proof and puncture proof bags/containers.

8) The bags/containers must contain properly sealed labels with date, name and address of the health care establishment.

9) The health care establishment must not store waste beyond 48 hrs.and if necessary,it must seek permission from the prescribed authority. However, as far as possible, storage beyond 48 hrs must be avoided, by making special arrangement with disposal agency.

10) The government should institute awards for safe hospital waste management.

Conclusion

The growing population has necessitated the growth of a number of health care establishments. In India the health sector is dominated by the private sector. The better health care facility offered by this sector has also raised the need for better management of clinical waste or biomedical waste.

The waste generated by the health care establishment includes a wide range of material like needles and syringes, soiled dressings, body parts, diagnostic samples, blood, chemicals, pharmaceuticals, medical devices and radioactive materials etc.

Biomedical waste management a major issue and concern not only to hospitals, nursing home, authorities, but also to the environment and law enforcement agencies, and the public in general.

The greatest risk of biomedical waste is from the infectious and sharp components of the waste because to health care workers handling waste and can contract HIV or AIDS, Hepatitis B and C.

These wastes pose risk to uninfected population if it comes in contact with it. Thus, it is essential that, the biomedical waste is properly handled segregated and is properly disposed.

The Government of India took a major step by enacting The Biomedical Waste (Management and Handling) Rules, 1998. Under Section 6 and 25 of Environmental Protection Act 1986, The rule deals with the generation/handling/treatment/disposal of Bio Medical Waste.

India is among very few countries which have specific biomedical waste laws in practice. The state government plays an important role in the implementation of biomedical rules as health is a subject matter under state list.

The health care establishment plays an important role in the biomedical waste management as they are generator of biomedical waste and are responsible in collecting segregating, storing and disposing it. The concept of Biosafety is fundamentally a preventive concept is an important concept in this matter.

It includes taking steps and measures to prevent infection to all medical, nursing and paramedical workers as well as by patients, attendants, ancillary staff and administrators in a hospital. The concept also includes taking measures to damage to the environment and uninfected pollution.

A Common Biomedical Waste Treatment Facility (CBWTF) is an important and cost effective way to treat and dispose biomedical waste. The installation of individual treatment facilities by small healthcare units requires comparatively high capital investment.

Apart from it, it requires separate manpower and infrastructure development for proper operation and maintenance of treatment systems. The Common Biomedical Waste Treatment Facility (CBWTF) is an answer to these important problems.

The Central Pollution Control Board (CPCB) has prescribed guidelines for Common Biomedical Waste Treatment Facilities as well as for the design and construction of Incinerators.

The State Government takes necessary steps to monitor the disposal of biomedical wastes through the State Pollution Control Boards (SPCBs)/Pollution Control Committees (PCCs) in the Union Territories, as per the provisions made under the Biomedical Waste (Management & Handling) Rules, 1998.

The need for proper biomedical waste management has gained importance in recent years with the growth private health care sector in India. Technology is playing a major role in bringing quality in healthcare, be it better nursing communication systems, patient monitoring devices or tele-medicine to provide a low cost diagnosis to remote patients, etc.

The concept of medical tourism, where hospitals of specialized nature will sooner or later come to light needs special attention. In this scenario a separate and autonomous department of the Government with penal powers is the need of the time to deal with biomedical waste management in India.

In Maharashtra, Maharashtra Pollution Control Board (MPCB) enforces these Rules by

- Authorization of HCEs for generation and handling of BMW
- Authorization of CBMWTDFs for collection, treatment and disposal of BMW
- Periodic inspection and audit of the "system" to ensure compliance with the law.
- Taking action for non-compliance.
- Carrying out inventorization of BMW to report the status
- Undertaking awareness programs at HCEs

In order to know whether all relevant legal provisions are being followed by the HCEs in Satara, and to find out the difficulties and problems in implementing these rules The researcher has undertaken this Minor Research Project on this topic, which is approved by Shivaji University and UGC and is funded by UGC.

The present study is conducted in Satara city. Hence it is limited to, all health care establishments within the boundaries of the Satara Municipal Council. Satara Municipal Corporation has divided the area of the Satara city into 39 wards (Parabhag) for governance and representation.

Health care establishment, especially hospitals in Satara City, were selected randomly by applying the simple random sampling method. Questioner, Interview and observation techniques have been used for collection of data. A questioner sheet was given to selected hospitals. Few in depth case studies have been conducted to collect detailed information about implementation of legal norms and difficulties if any in their compliance.

In Satara, Association of Hospital Owners (AHO) along with CBMWTDFs, namely, NATURE IN NEED and Indian Medical Association (IMA) have arranged for simple, feasible, and environmentally friendly solutions for BMW management at different hospital routes for every type of biomedical waste as per the BMW (Management and Handling) Rules 1998 as amended in 2011.

Former President of AHO, Dr Sandip Shrotri and President of AHO, Dr Amita Mahajani and the authority of CBMWTDF operator Shri A. B. Jadhav and Sagar Jadhav have developed the coherent scheme for biomedical waste management in Satara City, where the biomedical waste is collected by employees of Nature in Need and is transported to and disposed at the CBMWTDF Centre at Songoan near Satara City as per the legal provisions and rules.

CBMWTDF, Nature in Need, Satara has Incinerator, shredder, Autoclaving machine, sterilization tank, Disinfectant Tank etc. and is substantially following the guidelines prescribed by the Central Pollution Control Board and Maharashtra Pollution Control Board from time to time regarding collection, transportation and disposal of biomedical waste.

Waste audits has been made mandatory for renewal of Consent to Operate. This has ensured an increase in credibility of CBMWTDF Nature in Need and better Health, Safety and Environmental compliance from employees from HSEs in Satara city. The majority of health care establishments in Satara city are following of Biomedical Waste (Management and handing) Rules, 1998

Glossary

BMW	BioMedical Waste
BMW Rules	Biomedical Waste (Management and Handling) Rule, 1998 (as amended to date)
CBMWTDF	Common Bio Medical Waste Treatment and Disposal Facility
CPCB	Central Pollution Control Board
CO	Carbon Monoxide
CO2	Carbon Dioxide
DG	Diesel Generator
EC	Environmental Clearance
ETP	Effluent Treatment Plant (ETP)
EPA	Environment (Protection) Act, 1986 (as amended to date)
Facility	(Hazardous Waste)
GPS	Global Positioning System
HCE	Health Care Establishments
HCFs	Health Care Facilities
HCl	Hydrochloric Acid
HW (M, H & TM) Rules	Hazardous Waste (Management, Handling & Transboundary

KM	Kilometer
KW	Kilowatt Movement) Rules
MHz	Mega Hertz
MoEF	Ministry of Environment & Forests
MSPCB	Maharashtra State Pollution Control Board
NOx	Oxides of Nitrogen
O2,	Oxygen
PCC	Pollution Control Committee
PLC	Programmable logical control
RO	Regional Office/ Officer of MPCB
SPCB	State Pollution Control Board
TSDF	Treatment, Storage and Disposal
TOC	Total Organic Carbon
VOCs	Volatile Organic Compounds

ANNXURE A

QUESTIONNAIRE

Questionnaire prepared for doctors and health care establishments

"Implementation of Biomedical Waste (Management and Handling) Rules, 1998 By Hospitals in Satara City"

Questioner

Instructions: - * Please tick mark the answer/Write in the place provided.

* You may tick mark more than one answer if appropriate.

* This information will be kept confidential and will be used only for the academic and research purposes.

1) **Name of the Hospital/Clinic**

   _____

   —

2) **Number of beds**

   _____

3) **Name of the Doctor**

   _____

4) Kind of waste generated and approximate quantity per day

   a) Human Anatomical Waste(Human tissues, Body Parts)
      YES [ ]   NO [ ]

   b) Animal Waste
      YES [ ]   NO [ ]

   c) Microbiology & Biotechnology waste
      YES [ ]   NO [ ]

   d) Waste Sharps (Needles, Syringes, etc.)
      YES [ ]   NO [ ]

   e) Discarded Medicines & Cytotox in Drugs
      YES [ ]   NO [ ]

   f) Solid Waste   YES [ ]   NO [ ]
      (Items Contaminated with blood & Body fluids including cotton Dressings, etc.)

   g) Solid Waste   YES [ ]   NO [ ]
      (Disposable items like tubings, catheters IV Sets, etc.)

   h) Liquid Waste   YES [ ]   NO [ ]

   i) Incineration Ash   YES [ ]   NO [ ]

   j) Chemical Waste (Chemical used in disinfections etc.)
      YES [ ]   NO [ ]

Total Biomedical Waste generated per month _____Kg.

5) Method of disposal of Biomedical Waste by the hospital/clinic

    a) Disinfection and sterilization   YES ☐   NO ☐

    b) Distruction/Shredding   YES ☐   NO ☐

    c) Chemical treatment   YES ☐   NO ☐

    d) Microwaving   YES ☐   NO ☐

    e) Autoclaving   YES ☐   NO ☐

    f) Incineration   YES ☐   NO ☐

    g) Deep burial   YES ☐   NO ☐

    h) Disposal in secured landfill   YES ☐   NO ☐

    i) Use of common Bio Medical Waste Treatment & Disposal facility   YES ☐   NO ☐

6) Name & Address of common treatment & disposal of Biomedical Waste Facility Operator
_____
_____
_____

7) Is authorization from Pollution Control Board taken?
   YES [   ]   NO [   ]

8) State the date of latest renewal from Common Biomedical Waste Treatment and Disposal Facility
_____
___

9) Is infectious Biomedical Waste separated from General Waste?
   YES [   ]   NO [   ]

10) What container is used?
    Single Container [   ]   Different Container As Per Colour Code [   ]

11) At what point the biomedical waste is segregated as per colour code
    a) At generation of waste [   ]
    b) Storage [   ]
    c) Transportation [   ]
    d) Treatment & Disposal [   ]

12) Is the bag / container filled with waste for more than 3/4th capacity?
    YES [   ]   NO [   ]

13) How frequently the biomedical waste is removed?

Everyday ☐   Less than 48 Hrs. ☐   More than 48 Hrs. ☐

14) If untreated waste is stored beyond 48 hours is the permission obtained from authority?

    YES ☐   NO ☐   Not Applicable ☐

15) Where is the waste stored before it is removed from hospital/clinic?

_____

_____

16) Who removes the biomedical waste?
    a) From point of generation for intermediate storage.
- i. Doctor ☐
- ii. Wardboy / Nurse ☐
- iii. Anxiliary /other staff ☐
- iv. Sanitary Staff ☐

    b) For final disposal outside the hospital campus/clinic.
- I. Doctor ☐
- II. Wardboy/ Nurse ☐
- III. Anxiliary /other staff ☐
- IV. Sanitary Staff/Guard ☐

17) Is there any chance of unauthorized reuse or resale of the discarded items by anyone within or outside the premises?

YES ☐   NO ☐   Don't Know ☐

18) Is the container labeled (wash proof & prominently visible) according to Sec. IV of the rules with date, name, address, phone of the sender & receiver?

YES ☐   NO ☐

19) Is the information about labeling and color coding of the container displayed at prominent places near container?

YES ☐   NO ☐

20) Is waste collection timing & duty charts displayed / informed to waste collectors / supervisors?

YES ☐   NO ☐

21) Dose the container has Biohazards or Cytotoxic Symbol on it?

YES ☐   NO ☐

22) Whether Puncture proof plastic bag is used for collection of sharps etc?   YES ☐   NO ☐

23) Is there any policy about measures to be taken during accident/emergency regarding biomedical waste?

YES ☐   NO ☐

24) What is the cost involved / charges paid for biomedical waste disposal Rs. _____/month.

25) Is the information and training about the health hazards of biomedical waste and concerned rules given to the staff responsible for handling the same?
YES ☐   NO ☐

26) What safety measures are taken for medical/paramedical/cleaning & transportation staff?

    a) Protective gloves, aprons, masks, etc.   YES ☐   NO ☐

    b) Provision of disinfectant, soap, etc.   YES ☐   NO ☐

    c) Provision of wash area   YES ☐   NO ☐

    d) Regular medical check up   YES ☐   NO ☐

27) Is the record of generation, collection, transportation and disposal of biomedical waste kept in the register?   YES ☐   NO ☐

28) Is the annual report sent to pollution control board before 31 Jan. every year? YES ☐ NO ☐

29) What are the difficulties faced in implementing the biomedical waste rules?

_____
_____

_____
_____

30) What are your suggestions/comments with regard to prevention/minimization & control of biomedical waste hazards to human health & environment?

_____
_____
_____

Signature and Name of Doctor giving information

Name_____

Signature

Seal

Observations

_____
_____
_____
_____
_____

Annexure B

INTERVIEW QUESTIONNAIRE

Interview questionnaire prepared for Common Bio Medical Waste treatment Facility

Questioner

Instructions: - * Please tick mark the answer/Write in the place provided.

* You may tick mark more than one answer if appropriate.

* This information will be kept confidential and will be used only for the academic and research purposes.

1. **Name & Address of the common Bio Medical Waste Treatment Facility**

   _____

   Name of operator of a Bio Medical Waste Facility

   _____

2. **First grant of authorization from Pollution Control Board**

   _____

3. **Date of latest renewal**

   _____

4. Was the authorization suspended anytime?   YES ☐
   NO ☐   If Yes, During _____

5. Is the annual report sent before 31ˢᵗ Jan. every year to the Pollution control Board?
   YES ☐   NO ☐

6. Is the record related to handling of Bio Medical Waste kept in a register?
   YES ☐   NO ☐

7. Did any accident during transportation or handling of Bio Medical waste occurred in the past?
   YES ☐   NO ☐

8. If Yes was the accident reported to the Pollution Control Board in Form III?
   YES ☐   NO ☐

9. What kind of Bio Medical Waste Handling is done by you?
       a) Collection / Reception   ☐
       b) Storage   ☐
       c) Transport   ☐
       d) Treatment   ☐
       e) Disposal   ☐

10. What kind of vehicles are used for transportation of Bio Medical Waste?

    _____

    ____

    Total Nos. _____

11. What kind of containers /bags are used for transportation of Bio Medical Waste?

    Single Container [____] Separate Container [____] As per Color Code [____]

12. Are the container/bags labeled with (Washproof&Promently Visible) details given in Sc. III & Sc. IV?

    YES [____] NO [____]

    Do containers have Biohazards or Cytotoxic?

    YES [____] NO [____]

    Is there any chance of unauthorized reuse or resale of discarded items by any one during handling of Bio Medical Waste by you?

    YES [____] NO [____] Don't'Know [____]

13. What kind of staff is employed for the work? Give designation/category and No. of employees?

_____
    _____
_____
    _____
_____
    _____

14. What care is taken to prevent accident/improper handling of Bio Medical Waste?

_____
    _____
_____
    _____
_____
    _____

15. Do you provide safety measures to worker against operational health hazards?

    YES [_____] NO [_____]

16. Is vehicle transporting Bio Medical Waste covered and secured

YES [_____] NO [_____]

17. Is the interior of container smooth without sharp edges which can be easily washed and disinfected?

YES ☐ NO ☐

18. What standards for waste autoclaving are followed by you?

    a) Temperature ☐

    b) Pressure ☐

    c) Autoclave residence time ☐

19. How is recording of operational parameters maintained?

20. What Standards are followed by you for Microwaving?

21. What Standards are followed by you for deep burial?

22. Give brief description of method of treatment & disposal by you?

23. State the category & quantity of waste (category wise) handled per month by you?

24. What are the difficulties faced by you in implementing the Bio Medical Waste rules?

_____

_____

25. What are your suggestions/comments with regard to prevention minimization & control of Bio Medical Waste hazards to human health & environmental?

International Publication, peer reviewed by Lawbright.
http://lawbright.in/editorial-board.html

www.ingramcontent.com/pod-product-compliance
Lightning Source LLC
Chambersburg PA
CBHW070302190526
45169CB00001B/499